TRAVELING *Through* GRIEF

TRAVELING

Through

GRIEF

Learning to Live Again
after the Death of a Loved One

Susan J. Zonnebelt-Smeenge, R.N., Ed.D.
and
Robert C. DeVries, D.Min., Ph.D.

BakerBooks
Grand Rapids, Michigan

Published by Baker Books
a division of Baker Publishing Group
P.O. Box 6287, Grand Rapids, MI 49516-6287
www.bakerbooks.com

Printed in the United States of America

Library of Congress Cataloging-in-Publication Data
Zonnebelt-Smeenge, Susan J., 1948–
    Traveling through grief : learning to live again after the death of a loved one / Susan J. Zonnebelt-Smeenge and Robert C. DeVries.
      p. cm.
    Includes bibliographical references (p.   ).
    ISBN 10: 0-8010-6676-X (pbk.)
    ISBN 978-0-8010-6676-4 (pbk.)
    1. Bereavement—Religious aspects—Christianity. 2. Grief—Religious aspects—Christianity. 3. Bereavement—Psychological aspects. 4. Grief. I. DeVries, Robert C., 1942– II. Title.
    BV4905.3.Z67 2006
    248.8'66—dc22
                                                2006010301

Rarely does a person experience
the richness of the love,
the depth of the support,
and the strength of the encouragement
we receive from our parents

William G. Zonnebelt

and

Norma J. Zonnebelt

to whom we dedicate this book
with our deepest love and gratitude
for who and what they are to us.

Contents

Preface

Writing a book that will speak to the head and heart of a person torn apart by the death of a loved one is a tremendous challenge. Both of us have experienced heart-wrenching grief through the deaths of our first spouses, the deaths of brothers and grandparents, and, in Bob's case, through the death of parents. Some people want to read their way through grief. Others want to focus primarily on the emotions of grief. Still others try to avoid grief altogether—to run from it or hide from its devastating power. Our challenge is to speak not only to the heart of someone who has been torn by grief but also to the griever's head, because we firmly believe that people need to be active and intentional about their grief in order to heal. We want to say a word that may have some healing power and to cast a vision of a life that can be fulfilling and rewarding again once a person has completed their journey *through* grief.

Reading a book on grief can be difficult because it will force you to deal with some "tough stuff." If you are the one grieving, we commend you for your desire to read this short book, which is divided into digestible sections that hopefully will provide you with a positive outlook as well as a number of suggestions for managing your grief journey. In many ways this book is appropriate for a wide variety of losses that cut to the heart and impact your life, such as the breakup of a significant relationship or marriage, the loss of a job, the loss of health, or the loss of a pet. The central focus of this book, however, is specifically the death of a loved one, and we leave it to the reader to apply these principles and suggestions to other situations.

We have written three other books on the topics of dying, death, and grief. *Getting to the Other Side of Grief: Overcoming the Loss of a Spouse* addresses the grief journey following the death of a spouse. *The Empty Chair: Handling Grief on Holidays and Special Occasions* is a shorter book focused on managing those special days when the absence of a loved one is especially felt—days like Christmas, birthdays, the anniversary of the death, or any other time that was special in one's relationship with the deceased. Our third book, entitled *Living Fully in the Shadow of Death: Assurance and Guidance to Finish Well*, deals with the need to prepare for one's death, whether one is healthy or ill, young or old. The book is an extensive guide to all of the preparations a person should make emotionally, relationally, medically, financially, legally, and spiritually to face death. The book you are now reading takes its place in the series of our writing on death and bereavement as a resource on the grieving process following the death of someone you have loved—whether that is a parent, child, sibling, spouse, grandparent, or friend.

As in all our other books, we approach the subject from both a mental health and a Christian spiritual perspective, each contained in separate sections. Most readers will want to read both coordinated sections throughout the book, but even those who prefer not to read Christian meditations will benefit from reading the mental health perspective. Susan is a licensed clinical psychologist at Pine Rest Christian Mental Health Services (Grand Rapids, Michigan), and Bob is an ordained pastor and Professor Emeritus of Church Education at Calvin Theological Seminary (Grand Rapids, Michigan). Following the deaths of our first spouses in 1994 and 1993 respectively, we married each other in 1997 and have a blended family of four adult children with their spouses, and five grandchildren.

Acknowledgments

*F*inding the words that will provide the most help and comfort to someone who is grieving is a difficult task. When people are confronted by death, most often their response is simply "I don't know what to say!" So we want to say something helpful, and this book is one way for us to give expression to the grief journey. While the words are ours, several others have provided their expertise and perspective by reading the manuscript and offering advice.

Our parents, Bill and Norma Zonnebelt, and our daughter Sarah Byrd, a teacher, read the book as previous and prospective grievers to ensure our language was clear and understandable and laced with a sensitive and caring tone.

Both Patricia Cassell, a nurse and social worker, and C. J. Weidaw, a nurse and psychologist, as well as being our friends, offered their editorial and counseling insights in reviewing the final edition. Doug and Carol Luther, co-facilitators with us of a younger widowed support group and Carol also as the former director of the Greater Grand Rapids Widowed Persons Services, lent their wisdom as people well versed in grief both personally and professionally.

Our appreciation is also given to Bob Hosack, senior acquisitions editor, for his trust in the quality of our work, and to Kristin Kornoelje, assistant managing editor, trade books, for her editorial services ensuring the clarity of our message. We also want to thank the entire staff at Baker Publishing Group for their continued support of our writing on the topics of dying, death, and grief. While these are usually not comfortable topics for people to read about, we commend Baker Publishing Group for their commitment to educating and providing support for two of the most painful experiences in life—dying and grieving.

Susan J. Zonnebelt-Smeenge

Robert C. DeVries

"Death, like a fire, devastates, destroys.
Death seems to leave nothing but ashes
in its wake. Landmarks are destroyed.
A sense of hopelessness overwhelms. We
are not certain whether we can find our
bearings again. How will we ever navigate
this darkness?"[1]

"Grief is a tidal wave that overtakes
you, smashes down upon you with an
unimaginable force, sweeps you up into
its darkness, where you tumble and crash
against undefinable surfaces, only to
be thrown out on an unknown beach,
bruised, reshaped and unwittingly better
for the wear. . . . Grief will make a new
person out of you, if it doesn't kill you in
the making."[2]

One

Detour Ahead!

THE MENTAL HEALTH PERSPECTIVE

Oh No! A Detour! Grief Reroutes My Life's Journey

Life is a journey. We are born, we live our life, and we die. We are heading somewhere. We have goals and purposes, and we need some sort of road map to reach these goals. When we get up in the morning, we make our plans for the day. We set objectives for the week and for the coming months. We sign a thirty-year mortgage because we have some confidence that our job will generate the income, our health will prevail, and we can achieve the goal of living comfortably.

But sometimes things go wrong. Our course gets rerouted. Something happens, and our plans don't always work out. Economic downturns jeopardize our jobs. Relationships change. Marriages may fail. We experience losses, and as a result we have to change our plans and alter our goals. The journey changes; we are faced with a detour; we have to adjust. Researchers suggest that adjusting to the death of a loved one is probably the biggest adjustment we'll need to make in our lives. This book focuses on grief following the death of a person you loved (although many of the principles also relate to losses in general), how grief changes your life's journey, what the grief experience is like, and how you can use this forced detour called grieving to develop a revised life course that can become rich and rewarding again.

Grief causes a major detour on your life's journey because it is a natural response on your part to loss. Life ends; grieving the death of your loved one begins. Perhaps you are saying to yourself, "I have been grieving already!" because your loved one experienced an extended illness that led to death. Loved ones surrounding the dying person do grieve losses of function as the person is no longer able to do what he or she was previously able to do. We would contend that grieving those functional losses does not replace the need to grieve the person's actual death. No one can grieve the physical absence of the person until he or she actually dies.

Grief doesn't wait for you to invite it into your life when someone you love has died. It happens automatically and universally. Now, with the death of your loved one, you are *forced* to travel a detour rather than your intended route. You generally don't choose a route that you know will have a detour. You probably try to avoid detours, at almost any cost. In this book we use the analogy of your life as being on a road trip, and now, with the death of your loved one, you are forced to travel the detour of grieving.

Why Does Grief Happen?

Why does grief occur when someone dies? There are three primary reasons why this grief experience is happening to you:

1. *Because you loved that person.* Loving someone means that you were attached to him or her and cared deeply about that person. Hopefully the relationship and feelings were reciprocal. You knew each other well—what lay at each other's hearts.
2. *Because you formed a relationship with that person.* You likely experienced an emotional inter-

weaving with the other person—he or she was someone you could count on and with whom you had connected. You probably gave to and received many things from that relationship. Perhaps there were physical aspects you will miss—the hugs and touches, or if you were married, the sexual intimacy. Even if your relationship wasn't the healthiest or most satisfying, that doesn't mean you won't grieve. You still experience a loss.

3. *Because some part of your lifestyle was affected by your loved one's presence.* You grieve not only the person's death but also the end of the life you had lived with that person. That includes all you did together and all that came as a result of having that person in your life. No matter what role the person played in your life, you are now forced to recognize that your life will change dramatically in those areas that involved that person.

How Do I Get Rid of the Pain and Get Back to "Normal"?

Grief needs an *active, intentional decision* to face the pain of the loss. We are amazed at the number of people who seem to let grief overtake them and then passively wait, thinking grief will eventually end without doing anything to help end it. We think this is because they don't know what to do. Using our own personal experiences and our professional knowledge of the grief process, we would like to help you work *through* grief.

Take, for example, a person who falls and breaks a leg. The broken leg will hurt. The person does not decide to experience pain—it comes naturally. The pain of grief comes just as naturally when a loved one dies. But just as the physical pain of a fracture usually motivates a person to do something about the injury (like going to the doctor, taking pain medication, getting a cast applied, or having surgery), hopefully the pain of grief will motivate you to do something to help you along the grief process.

The basic premise of this book is that a grieving person needs to *intentionally* engage in healthy and helpful actions to address their grief in order to move through grieving and discover a fulfilling life once again. The passing of time is a necessary element in the grief process, but it's not enough by itself. Healthy grieving takes *deliberate, intentional actions* coupled with *time* in order for a person to effectively heal after a death.

With a loved one's death, grief often rolls over you like an overpowering wave sucking you down to the bottom and making you feel like there is nothing left—familiar landmarks are gone with no reason to go on. It's a very overwhelming and painful experience to have to deal with, so we want you to understand a little more clearly what your grief will probably look and feel like. This grief journey is often described as a slow process ultimately moving in a positive direction but coupled with intermittent "lows" or "valleys" that may seem like a step backward. Remember, grieving is not a consistently upward linear process. Grief is more like waves on the ocean—the waves ebb and flow as storms, winds, and tides change. Grieving takes *at least* a year, and most likely a few more, to complete. That's because finding out who you are without your loved one takes time and hard work.

Your grief journey is unique, and there is no uniform way to grieve because of all the individual factors in your life in contrast to others, such as your own and your deceased loved one's personalities, the type of relationship you had together, the type of death your loved one experienced, your present individual life circumstances, and how soon you began doing intentional grief work. But regardless of all your individual life circumstances, there are five universal components to grief that you may well encounter on your grief detour. Research has clearly demonstrated that the experience of grief triggers aspects of all of the following five responses for almost everyone.

1. *Physical.* Changes occur in eating and exercise patterns, frequently with a lack of desire to do either. Sleep becomes problematic and is often interrupted by thoughts of the deceased. A bereaved person is usually at a higher risk for illness and even death because the stress of loss and the physical and emotional drain of grieving lowers one's immune system, making good self-care so important.

2. *Emotional.* A grieving person often experiences a flood of emotions including, of course, sadness, but also anger, fear, anxiety, guilt, regret, relief, loneliness, and a myriad of other feelings, many of which seem overwhelming and worrisome.

3. *Cognitive.* The way a person thinks is usually affected by grief. Some people may make impulsive decisions or not be able to make any decisions at all. The advice to wait at least one year before making major decisions is well founded. Memory is disrupted, especially short-term; a person may not remember from one moment to the next what he or she was getting ready to do or who called on the phone. The ability to focus and concentrate is often disrupted. All of this often combines into a fear that the bereaved person is "going crazy."

4. *Behavioral.* Typical patterns of behavior are often disrupted. A person may go from one extreme to the

other in their behaviors. For example, he or she may either refuse to leave their house or fight against going home. The individual may have a difficult time returning to work or may throw himself or herself completely into work in an effort to distract from the grief experience. The bereaved person may lack motivation to accomplish even routine household responsibilities like opening the mail or doing the laundry. Apathy, withdrawal, and procrastination are also common occurrences.

5. *Spiritual.* Invariably, questions about one's spiritual faith and continuing purposes in life are raised by the death of a loved one. Even if a person is not particularly religious, death may force him or her to examine their belief about life after death. If a bereaved person has an active faith, that faith may be challenged, changed, or confirmed in regard to a multitude of questions frequently asked, including why God allowed this to happen.

Using the Tasks of Grief to Deal with Your Loss

Death certainly interrupts life's plans. The time you planned to spend together in retirement, or the hopes and dreams of seeing a child grow up and have a career and family are now out of the question. Maybe you feel like an orphan without a parent (even if you are an adult), or you miss the camaraderie of a sibling or valued friend. This isn't what you had hoped or intended for your life's journey. How can you make the most of this unwanted detour? How will you do this thing called grieving?

As you continue reading this book, you will be introduced to five "tasks" that can structure your journey through this grief detour. These tasks work together, the way a physician may do a number of things to help a broken leg heal. They will help you think about and do things that constitute healthy ways to work through your grief so you can begin to heal and reconstruct your life's route.

So what do we mean by "tasks," and how can they help? We intentionally use the word *tasks* (as do many others in the field of grief studies)[3] because of the connotation of "things that have to be done." You may be the kind of person who makes lists of things that need to be accomplished. You do a task, check it off, and move to another task. Many of these tasks may be interrelated but with no particular order to them. They are simply things that need to be done at some given point.

Tasks of grieving are something like that. These tasks are five interrelated goals that need to be accomplished or experienced for a person to move through the grief process into a full, healthy, and rewarding life following the death of a loved one (whether that is a spouse, parent, sibling, child, or friend). They are not sequential in the sense that one task needs to be completed before you begin another. In fact, they are complexly interrelated like a fine symphony, with parts of one task being worked on simultaneously with others. They are not the type of tasks that can be completed quickly or all at once—these tasks are integral to your entire grieving process.

This grief process is like putting a complex puzzle together. There are as many ways of accomplishing this as there are individuals doing it. However, there *are* designated puzzle pieces to be used in specific relationship to others. Only when the puzzle is complete can a person sit back and appreciate the entire picture for what it is and declare it to be finished. That is also true of the grief process—it is an individual journey, yet there are the five specific tasks with corresponding behaviors that you need to address to help you move through your grief detour.

So what are these tasks that are necessary to heal from grief?

- *First*, you need to accept the reality that your loved one has died and is unable to return. This may seem obvious, but emotionally accepting the reality of the death can be a tremendous challenge.

- *Second*, you need to express all your emotions associated with the death. Keeping the emotions "bottled up" inside yourself can complicate your grief journey.
- *Third*, you need to sort through and identify the memories of your loved one and find a place to store them so you can begin to move on. This task basically means that because your loved one is no longer present—no longer a dynamic and active part of your ongoing journey—you need to make him or her a vital and rich memory of your past life.
- *Fourth*, identify who you are independent of your deceased loved one. If you experienced the death of your second parent, are you now an orphan? If a child died, how do you answer the question, "How many children do you have?" When your spouse dies, are you still married? Or widowed? Or single? Reworking your sense of identity is a critical aspect of your grief journey.
- *Finally*, the grief detour requires that you begin to reinvest in your life in a way that is consistent with your reshaped sense of identity—determining your own personal interests and desires at this point in your life.

These five tasks combine to help you travel to the other side of your grieving in a healthy and satisfying way. In the following chapters we will explain each of these tasks in much more detail so you know how to work through them in order to heal.

THE SPIRITUAL PERSPECTIVE

Detour Ahead—Where Was God?

> **Genesis 2:16–17:** "You are free to eat from any tree in the garden; but you must not eat from the tree of the knowledge of good and evil, for when you eat of it you will certainly die."

- Does God *cause* a person's death or *allow* it? What is the difference? Why do bad things happen to Christians?

Did you ever think of the Garden of Eden as a heavenly smorgasbord? God created all the fruits and vegetables, placed them in the Garden, and with a broad sweep of his hand said to Adam and Eve something like, "Go ahead, eat. It's all yours. Eat until you are full." Perhaps your life felt blessed like that before your loved one died. Even if you had some struggles, you were still relatively content, motivated by a vision of what might be down the road. However, God did add one condition to what he said to Adam and Eve. "Just don't eat from that one tree over there! You have hundreds of others, but that one is off limits. You eat from it, you will certainly die." But they yielded to temptation and ate from it, and death became a reality.

In order to understand the death of your loved one, you really need to understand this story in Genesis. To put it bluntly, God did *not* make the stipulation to refrain from eating from the tree because he *wanted* us to die. In his very nature God is a loving and merciful God, but he's also a just God. He loved his creation and, most of all, Adam and Eve. But he also created the world and the human race with certain laws and rules to follow. God gave Adam and Eve a command not to eat from one tree in the middle of the garden. If they disobeyed, the consequence would be death. This was the warning label on the bottle of a dangerous substance: if you eat this, you will die. God is not the villain in this story, he is the hero. Even though God warned them not to, Adam and Eve did it to themselves, and they (as our human parents) did it to us as well.

Maybe you're wondering if your loved one died as a direct punishment for personally doing something wrong or sinful. That is probably not the case. It is true that all of us sin and need to repent. But the primary reason your loved one died is because we all die. As a result of Adam and Eve's sin we now collectively suffer the consequences of brokenness.

Each one of us will still have to die a physical death. However, God stepped in. In Genesis 3:15 he promised that the "seed" of the woman would crush the head of the serpent. That means there will be victory over death! Death was not part of God's original creation, but once sin entered the world, God provided a final victory over death through the death and resurrection of Jesus Christ (1 Cor. 15:54).

Right now you still face the detour. Death is here to stay—at least until Christ returns. And with death comes grief. Hopefully, however, your visit to the grave will remind you of the disciples' Easter morning visit to Christ's empty grave. Your loved one's body is in the ground, but because of Christ's resurrection those who believed in Christ are already with God. Take comfort in that truth.

Prayer: Dear Lord, it doesn't seem fair that I have to suffer like this because of what Adam and Eve did so many years ago. But then, it doesn't seem fair that Jesus had to die on the cross because of the sin of all of us in this world either. Help me focus on his victory even while I am on this grief detour. *Amen*

Weak Faith and a Mustard Seed

> **Genesis 2:18:** *"The Lord God said, 'It is not good for the man to be alone. I will make a helper suitable for him.'"*

> **Matthew 17:20:** *"Truly I tell you, if you have faith as small as a mustard seed, you can say to this mountain, 'Move from here to there' and it will move. Nothing will be impossible for you."*

- **Why does God allow me to hurt like this? How can I have faith in God while I am grieving? How much faith do I need for the grief journey?**

God created us to have special relationships in our lives. The story of creation tells how God created Adam and Eve in a very close relationship with one another. God also created them to be in a wonderfully intimate relationship with him—so intimate that they walked with God in the Garden during the cool of the day (Gen. 3:8). But then it happened. They disobeyed God's command, which led to the consequence of death. And death leads to grief because a relationship has been severed. When someone you love dies, you hurt deeply because you were emotionally attached. You miss that person's laughter, insights, presence, and companionship. No one will ever replace that person in your life.

But this death also likely affects your relationship with God. In some ways you may feel his presence closer to you. In other ways, God may seem so very distant. Adam and Eve were afraid of God after they sinned. They heard God coming and hid in the bushes (Gen. 3:8). You may want to hide as well, or at least not want to be in his presence. Prayer may be tough. All you may want to do, especially during the early days and weeks of your grief, is shake your fist at God and wonder why he let this thing happen to you. Know that grieving people often have a hard time with their emotions toward God. They wonder how he could be a loving God and let this happen to them. Or they just turn their back on him for the time being.

Remember that thousands of years after Adam and Eve, we find Jesus (the second Adam) saying something about having such a small faith, like your faith might be right now—small as a mustard seed—but that with it you can move mountains. Even if you are hurt or angry with God, you hopefully still have that seed of faith within you. You still believe that God is there. You probably do, because you are still talking with him, asking him, "Why?" "Why now?" "Why him or her?"

You don't have to try to be a saint to get through grief. As a Christian you can still doubt or wonder why God allowed this all to happen. You may not like the answer that death is a necessary consequence because God is just and holy. But deep in your heart, all you need is a seed. A little mustard seed. God promises that you will eventually be able to move through this mountain of grief and reinvest in life fully and faithfully at the end of this detour. Know that he is already alongside of you in this process.

Prayer: Dear Lord, search my heart and find my faith, small as it may be right now—a mustard seed seemingly without a lot of potential. Water it with your Spirit and help it grow strong so that I can move through this mountain of grief to the other side. *Amen*

How Long, O Lord, Will I Grieve?

Psalm 13:1: "How long, O LORD? Will you forget me forever? How long will you hide your face from me?"

1 Thessalonians 4:13: "Brothers and sisters, we do not want you to be uninformed about those who sleep in death, so that you do not grieve like the rest, who have no hope."

- May I as a Christian grieve? How long will this pain of grief last? Can't I just give my grief to God and let him deal with it, or must I also do something?

Waiting is tough, especially if you are waiting for relief from pain, or waiting in a traffic jam, or waiting for a son or daughter to call. What is even more difficult is waiting for the pain of grief to subside. Sometimes it seems like the grief will never end. King David felt like God deserted him. You might feel the same way. Listen to the words of David and see if they aren't something like what you might be saying:

> How long, LORD? Will you forget me forever? How long will you hide your face from me? How long must I wrestle with my thoughts and day after day have sorrow in my heart? How long will my enemy triumph over me? Look on me and answer, LORD my God. Give light to my eyes, or I will sleep in death.
>
> Psalm 13:1–3

When overwhelmed by grief, crying out to God is normal. "How long, O Lord? How long?"

David, however, doesn't just cry or complain. In verses 3 and 4 he begins to reason with God. He knew that God had made promises to him, and now he is actually challenging God to keep his promises so that everyone who is watching him (his "enemies") won't have a reason to mock him. If the first conversation you have with God is "How long?" this psalm suggests that your next one begin with the words: "You promised!" What has God promised you while on your grief detour? *First*, God promised he would be with you for the entire journey, no matter what it encompasses or how long it lasts. Remember Psalm 23:4: "Even though I walk through the valley of the shadow of death, you are with me" (NIV). Notice it says you *do* walk through the valley, but God will go with you. *Second*, God promised you hope. You still go *through* the valley; you cannot avoid it. You really do grieve, but with hope (1 Thess. 4:13). That is the primary difference between a Christian's and a non-Christian's grieving process. First Corinthians 15:54 tells us that death is swallowed up in Christ's final victory. So there is death—an awful parting. But that's not all there is. Finally, a victory—eternal life— is promised to all who believe. So live in that hope for the future as well as the present and believe God's promise that he will be with you all the way—even on your grief detour.

So now, the final conversation David has with God in verses 5 and 6 is: "I still trust you!" That may be hard to say right now. Your cry may still be, "How long, O Lord?" But in that cry, remember God's promises—promises of his presence, hope, and a final victory. Then your faith can grow, and you will be able to say again, "I trust you, God. I really do."

Prayer: How long, O Lord? How long must this grief press down on me? You promised that you would never leave me. Restore my hope and give me a vision of tomorrow as well as support for today. Minute by minute I can get through this difficult valley, for my hope and trust is still in you. *Amen*

Two

No U-Turn
on Your Journey

THE MENTAL HEALTH PERSPECTIVE

The Grief Detour—Accepting the Reality of the Death

The first task of grief is that you *recognize and accept the fact that your loved one has died and is unable to return.* You may be able to comprehend your loved one's death in your mind, but emotionally you may find yourself searching for that person when you walk into your house or find yourself wanting to phone him or her with some news of the day. Yearning for your loved one's presence is a powerful force that frequently leads to dreams of that person, or thinking you saw or heard from that person, or sensing his or her presence around you. In your head you *know* your loved one has died, but in your heart you can't *believe* it yet. It will take considerable time for your heart (emotional level) to finally comprehend what your head (thinking level) has known—that this death really did happen, and it will change your life forever.

There is a mysterious connection between a grieving person's thoughts and feelings. We can think of no other time when the separation between the mind and the emotion is sharper than when you are dealing with the death of someone you love. The principle behind this first task of grief is simply that eventually both the mind and the heart must acknowledge the loss. It may seem like they do initially. You may say, "Of course I know he or she died," but that probably isn't your emotions talking, but rather your head. Approximately six to nine months following the death, many people experience a surprising, gut-wrenching emotional realization that the deceased person will never be back. That may be the case for you as well—both your mind and your heart realize that you will have to live the rest of your life without that person. Then you will probably be looking for answers to some very tough questions, such as, "How can I ever get my life back into balance without my loved one?"

Accepting the hard reality that your loved one has died and is never coming back is extremely painful but is absolutely necessary to the grief process. You still have your own life to live. But you will need to do some things that are very difficult—to do the "tough stuff" of grief to help you begin to accept the reality of your loved one's death.

Three principles serve as the foundation for this recommendation that you do this tough stuff. The *first* principle is that by taking small steps you will eventually get to the point of emotionally accepting the reality of the death, and then that reality will be less intimidating. This is called "desensitization." Take swimming, for example. Someone who is afraid of water can learn to swim if they are slowly exposed to it rather than being thrown into the lake from the deep end of the dock. Similarly, if you repeatedly take small steps to expose yourself to the reality of your loss, your fear of facing painful things and doing this tough stuff will diminish.

A *second* principle is that you use your senses to assimilate the reality of your loved one's death. For example, actually seeing the body of your loved one is a very important way to confront this reality. We often say, "Seeing is believing." If you haven't had the funeral yet, most funeral homes would be open to you helping prepare your loved one's body by bathing or dressing it, styling the person's hair, or applying the cosmetics if you wish to do so. By doing these things you are subtly forced to begin lining up your emotions with what your head has told you is true—namely, this person has died. That is painful and tough to realize. But we also believe that trying to make the process less difficult for you and your family is counterproductive to healthy grieving.

If you have been through the funeral already, find some way to focus on the reality of the death by replaying the funeral events in your mind. If someone had the foresight to take pictures, look at the ones of your loved one in the casket. You might also touch and smell their clothing or other belongings. Our senses (to see, hear, feel, smell, taste) help us understand what is happening around us. By replaying these images in your mind frequently, the reality of this person's death will begin to sink in. Many people think it would be better to avoid any circumstance that causes pain or unpleasantness. What they fail to recognize is that *facing painful situations is an integral part of the healing*. Actually using your senses to confront reality is a solid step on your journey toward accepting that your loved one is dead and that you will have to "let go" of that person.

A *third* principle is that someone who has died simply cannot return. This may seem so obvious that it doesn't have to be said. But as human beings, we often want to stay connected to our loved ones in almost any way possible. We don't want to let go. There may be some people who encourage you to "stay connected" and "continue bonds" with your loved one as if they were still present with you. (Some researchers and counselors currently promote this view.) We will talk more about this when we explain the third task of grief. Right now we simply want to say that in our view, you *can* stay connected to your loved one through your memories and through what you have become because of your relationship with that person. But we don't believe you can have an ongoing present relationship with someone who is dead.

This task requires you not only to accept the reality of the death but also to accept the permanent, concrete, physical dissolution of any relationship you had with the deceased person. A mother is no longer a mother to a deceased daughter, because that daughter is no longer here. A grandchild is no longer a grandchild to a deceased grandfather. A husband is no longer married to a deceased wife. Certainly, they can accurately say that they *were* a mother, a grandchild, or a husband to that deceased person, but the important point is that with the person's death the verb must now be moved to the past tense. The relationship is something that *was*, but *is* no more. That is why we strongly urge you not only to see the body of your loved one after he or she has died but also to watch the body being buried in the ground or the cremains being scattered. Then you can also visit the grave or scattering site to remember the internment and be reminded that the person is no longer physically present in your life.

The Effects of the Detour—Dealing with the Shock and Numbness

Initially, two of the most common companions on your grief detour are shock and numbness. If you have already said, "I just don't believe he or she is dead," then you know what we are talking about. The death is unbelievable, and yet in some ways very believable, creating a strange emotional sensation. As we have mentioned earlier, the connection between our minds (thoughts) and feelings (emotions) is very complex. The challenge of grief is that following the death of a loved one, our level of awareness is initially protected by shock and numbness, which are natural responses to this trauma. Even if you had anticipated the death because your loved one had been ill, the shock is still real. In many cases when a loved one has died suddenly and unexpectedly, the shock and numbness may be more intense and last longer than if the death were anticipated.

But no matter how the death occurred, all of those who are grieving experience some degree of this shock and numbness. Actually, this numbness helps to immediately shield a grieving person from the full force of grief and allows him or her to handle what they can at the time so it isn't even more overwhelming than it already seems. If you are grieving, be patient with yourself. Just as the pain of a physical injury will slowly diminish, so also will this shock and numbness decrease as you are able to more directly face the reality of your loss.

Specific Ways to Work on Your Grief

Things to Do Immediately

✚ First of all, take care of yourself physically. Grieving is exhausting. Remember, your physical health is more fragile while you are grieving. Keeping your body healthy is extremely important. Focus on that. Get a physical exam from your physician. Use the acronym

DEER[4] as a reminder of how you must take care of yourself during your grieving process.

D = Drink plenty of fluids (avoid more than a minimal amount of alcohol).

E = Eat at least three meals a day (even if you don't feel like it); maintain a balanced meal plan using the food pyramid for the recommended food groups.

E = Exercise—take a walk, ride your bike, or do something that keeps your body active. It may be difficult to get yourself going, so start small. Walk around your block, then gradually build up to walking between thirty to forty-five minutes at least four times a week.

R = Rest; although sleep may be difficult, remember that grief is physically as well as emotionally draining. Rest is critical to good self-care. You may need to get a medication for sleep from your physician if you continually feel exhausted and regularly have difficulty getting a good night's rest.

✚ Use the words *dead* and *died* to talk about your loved one rather than euphemisms like "gone," "passed away," "lost," or "in another or better place." The words *dead* and *died* may sound harsh or cold, but they will help you recognize the seriousness of what has happened and the finality of this person's death.

Things to Do Whether You Are Still Planning the Funeral Events or Recalling Them

✚ Have an open casket or at least see the body of your deceased loved one if at all possible. This can be done even if you decide on cremation. It is a myth that you will not be able to remember your loved one as he or she was when alive if you see them after they have died. Our minds are phenomenal in what they can assimilate. We can remember everything about that person even if the last image we had of him or her was in the casket. So add to your collection of memories the image of the person after he or she died. Ask someone to take pictures. This will help you accept the reality of the death both cognitively and emotionally. We realize that some people's bodies are not able to be recovered, and this may complicate grieving because it can obscure the reality of the death. If the funeral is over, recall what the person looked like dead and replay in your mind the various aspects of the funeral.

✚ Make certain the funeral events are not only a celebration of the person's life but also an acknowledgment that the person has died and will be missed. Expressions of sadness and grief that the person will no longer grace your life are very appropriate and beneficial to the grieving process.

✚ Schedule the visitation, the funeral, and the burial or scattering with time in between each so they don't become a blur of activity. By doing this you can better digest each event and allow more thoughts to be expressed and emotions to be released.

✚ Go to the graveside or where the cremains will be placed for an internment service. Say good-bye as you touch the casket or cremains. Stay at the graveside to watch the casket lowered into the ground, and then shovel dirt on the deceased's casket. This is the beginning of the hundreds of good-byes you will be saying while on this grief detour.

Things to Do throughout the Grief Detour

✚ If the person who died lived with you, return to your usual home environment as soon as you are able. This may be painful for you, but it is a critically important step of this task. Living in that environment without your loved one helps you begin to accept that this is now how things are.

✚ Look through your sympathy cards and listen to or view the funeral service. Copy over helpful sayings, poems, or Bible verses used in the funeral, sympathy cards, or supportive comments people made so you can refer to them frequently for comfort as you grieve.

✚ If you are the closest relative to the deceased, you are the one who needs to deal with all your loved one's clothes, favorite memorabilia, and possessions. You will have to deal with things like the sewing machine, fishing poles, toys, skis, a drawing table or workbench. Decide if you still want these things for yourself, and if so, where you want to put them. Claim them as your own—as "my skis" or "my worktable" rather than the deceased's. If you were married and are now widowed, work at using "I" or "my" rather than "ours." If you don't want some items, decide how you will dispose of them. Give some things to other grievers so they can remember your loved one in a tangible way, or donate them to a charity. Make a quilt from some favorite articles of clothing, or do something else creative with them as a keepsake. Remember, you don't need to do this all at once—you can take your time to smell the scent of your loved one's clothes or wear some of them if you want. But do plan to personally sort through the clothing, memorabilia, and mementoes yourself. Don't let others do it for you. Begin by looking at and touching items and gradually deciding what to do with the personal possessions. Doing this bit by bit or in layers can be helpful. If it has been a year since your loved one died, we recommend you formulate a plan to really begin working hard on this process—he or she is no longer alive and no longer needs these things. Most bereaved people tend to deal with all the belongings and mementoes within the first year or two. Doing this may be painful, but remember the premise—doing the painful tough stuff eventually brings healing. Put the items you want to keep in a remembrance box along with pictures and other valued mementoes to look at later, but otherwise gradually claim the territory (rooms, closets, or other special places) for yourself now. You are the new owner.

✚ Go to the library or area bookstore to find books on grieving that can assist you in the grieving process. It helps to know that others also struggled with the death of a loved one and what was helpful to them that you might try. Learn all you can about how to use this detour through grief to grow.

THE SPIRITUAL PERSPECTIVE

It's Not Only "Dust to Dust"

> **Genesis 3:19:** "... until you return to the ground, since from it you were taken; for dust you are and to dust you will return."

1 Corinthians 15:44: "*[The body] is sown a natural body, it is raised a spiritual body.*"

- **What has happened to my loved one now that he or she has died? Will he or she have a physical body? What kind of relationship can I have with my loved one? Will he or she be able to see me? What if I'm not sure that my loved one went to heaven?**

Accepting the reality of a loved one's death—how hard can that be? After all, you may have been at their bedside when death occurred, or you may have viewed the person lying in the casket. You may have been the one to throw flowers or dirt into the grave or scatter the cremains in a favorite place. To everyone else, it is obvious that your loved one has died—obvious to everyone except your heart!

Even when your emotions slowly begin to catch up with reality, you may wonder what has happened to your loved one now that he or she has died. Can this person still see me? What does he look like? How old is she in heaven? Is that birthmark still present? Is she still disfigured by arthritis?

The underlying question is really the question of the apostle Paul: "With what kind of body will they come?" (1 Cor. 15:35). God told Adam and Eve after they sinned that "for dust you are and to dust you will return" (Gen. 3:19). The physical body was formed from the earth, and God said that our bodies will now decompose and return to these earthly elements.

Paul compared our bodies to a seed. The seed, like a grain of wheat, decomposes and produces something new and wonderful. So it is with our bodies. What is perishable, weak, and "natural" is now raised imperishable, powerful, and "spiritual." Perhaps our bodies will be something like Jesus's following his resurrection. Everyone could still recognize him—his physical body seemed similar to what it was before his death. However, the Bible doesn't tell us much about what we will look like, how old we might be, and so on. But we will still have a body (Christ actually ascended into heaven with his physical body), although it will be a "spiritual body"—a term that is an oxymoron to most of us. For us, something is either physical or it is spiritual. It can't be both. Except in heaven. That is an exciting mystery to be fully revealed when we die.

Sometimes people are uncertain if a loved one may actually be in heaven. If you are facing doubts about that, you might find some comfort in knowing that God tells us that he will have mercy on those to whom he wants to have mercy (Rom. 9:15). He reminds us that we cannot really know the mind of God (Isa. 40:12–14) or what his final plans and decisions are. While the Bible is clear that salvation is in the name of Christ alone, and that faith is required for salvation, the Bible is also clear that one's faith can be very, very small. You don't know what transpired in your loved one's mind and heart immediately prior to death. Perhaps the most important thing to remember is that when you get to heaven, the issue of your loved one's final destiny will be settled, and whatever the conclusion of their life was, you will not experience any sadness because there is no sadness in heaven.

You may also wonder if your loved one can still see you. Based on our study of the Bible, we believe that people in heaven are not able to see anything on this earth. Seeing us on earth would spoil the spectacular experience for those who have died, for they would see us with our trials and difficulties. Death ends our earthly relationships, which is a painful realization that we will address later in this book. Jesus asked that we have the eye of faith to see beyond this grave and to know that when he returns, we will all be together around the throne of the risen Lamb of God.

Prayer: Dear Lord, give me the courage to see the grave of my loved one as the final resting place of their earthly body. But at the same time, give me the eye of faith to know that someday we all will live in heaven together

gathered around your throne, resurrected
with new, glorious spiritual bodies. *Amen*

Death—Life's Tragic Conclusion

> **Psalm 90:4–6:** *"A thousand years in your sight
> are like a day that has just gone by, or like a watch
> in the night. Yet you sweep people away in the
> sleep of death—they are like the new grass of the
> morning: In the morning it springs up new, but by
> evening it is dry and withered."*

- **Why is the death of my loved one so hard to
  accept? I thought God created us to live—why am I
  surrounded by death and grief?**

Look closely at the calligraphy on page 53.[5] After
you have studied it for a few moments, rotate the top of
the page to the left. Now what do you see? Then turn
it all the way to the right. Do you see another word?
We often use this calligraphy to demonstrate that life
and death are intricately related to each other. You
cannot have the one without the other. This was *not*
how God originally designed life. Adam and Eve's disobedience brought death into our world. The apostle
Paul makes that quite clear when he said, "Sin entered
the world through one man, and death through sin,

and in this way death came to all people, because all sinned" (Rom. 5:12). That is, of course, very sad news. Since the entrance of sin, life and death have been constant companions. Every birth begins a journey toward the grave.

We don't mean this to be depressing. God allows us to live a rich, full, and rewarding life between birth and death. Our life on earth is lived in the "meantime"—lived between Christ's ascension and his final return when death itself will be completely wiped out. The decisive battle has been won at Calvary and Easter. But the final peace treaty has not yet been signed. That will happen when Christ returns, and then we can claim eternal life with him.

The author of Psalm 90 compares us to grass. We spring up vital and energetic in the morning, but by nightfall we wither and fade away. We may live, says the psalmist, for seventy years, or perhaps eighty. But we won't live here forever. So the psalmist prays, "Satisfy us in the morning with your unfailing love, that we may sing for joy and be glad all our days. . . . May the favor of the LORD our God rest on us; establish the work of our hands for us" (Ps. 90:14, 17). In other words, help our life on earth to be profitable.

Do you know who wrote that psalm? It was Moses, who was hidden in the reeds of the Nile, raised by Pharaoh's household, was in exile as a murderer, was called by God to set his people free from bondage, met God face to face on the top of Mt. Sinai, and finished his days peering across the border into the promised land. A full life, to be sure, but one that ended in death. That is the reality. We live and we die, so that in Christ we may live forever. Moses's advice for those who are grieving is the words of Psalm 90:12: "Teach us to number our days, that we may gain a heart of wisdom."

Prayer: Dear God, death is so hard to understand and accept. Yet we know that death walks hand in hand with life itself. Teach me to know that even as my loved one has died, I must also be wise about how I will spend the rest of my time on this earth. Heal my grief, satisfy me with your unfailing love, and let your gracious favor rest on me. *Amen*

You Are Not Alone in Your Grief

> **Psalm 23:4:** *"Even though I walk through the darkest valley, I will fear no evil, for you are with me; your rod and your staff, they comfort me."*

- The hope for those grieving is that God will always be with you. How can I know that God is near me in my grief?

Death! Fear! Grief! How these words come crashing down on us when a loved one dies. Even for Christians, the pain of grief runs deep. No one seems to understand—sometimes especially those who say they do. Maybe their brother, or wife, or daughter died as well. But it wasn't the death of *your* loved one they experienced. This is different. *You* are now alone—separated by death from the person you loved deeply. No one, it seems, can really grasp the vastness of your pain and longing.

But now, listen to the quiet whisper in a refrain from Psalm 23. Even though this has all happened, even though death has come to your home, God is with you. He will comfort you.

Up to this point, our meditations have focused on accepting the reality of death. That is exactly how the psalmist begins: "Even though I walk through the valley of the shadow of death . . ." (Ps. 23:4 NIV). The Bible doesn't deny the reality of death. You and I shouldn't either, as ugly and traumatic as it may be.

But the psalm begins to swell with confidence. "I will fear no evil." That may be the boisterous declaration from a confident believer. On the other hand, it may also be a whispered reminder that you can have confidence in the face of uncertainty. It may be a resolution and prayer combined: "Please God, know that I don't want to be afraid of what lies ahead; release me from the power of this fear."

In the face of death we can easily vacillate between despair and hope. Grief surely overwhelms us. But we also cling to Christ, in whom we have placed our trust and confidence. This psalm reminds us that our trust is not misplaced. This whispered refrain ends with the phrase "Your rod and your staff, they comfort me" (Ps. 23:4). These are the shepherd's tools, and Jesus is the Good Shepherd. The shepherd uses the rod to protect his flock from predators. The staff, on the other hand, is the tool by which the shepherd gently guides the sheep, bringing them safely into the fold.

God's protective rod and guiding staff may not be clearly evident in the middle of your grief. You need to trust that they are there. The one thing you need now is the confidence of Psalm 23: "I will fear no evil, for you are with me; your rod and your staff, they comfort me"

(Ps. 23:4). Other friends and family members may offer some support. But they have their own lives to live. They will go back to their routines. But you are not alone in your grief. As you accept the reality of your loved one's death, focus on the one greater reality—God's presence with you. Remember the Good Shepherd who laid down his own life for his sheep. Let his rod and staff comfort you.

Prayer: My Father in heaven, I feel so alone, so overwhelmed in my grief. Let me have the confidence of this psalm to know that you are with me. Use your rod to chase away the evil threats from my spirit, and use your staff to guide me through this detour of grief. *Amen*

Three

Detours
Are Frustrating!

THE MENTAL HEALTH PERSPECTIVE

What to Do with All My Feelings: Being Real vs. Pretending

The second task of grief is that you *experience all the emotions associated with the death of your loved one.* Grief consists of a number of emotions that need to be honestly and freely expressed. If they are not acknowledged and become internalized, that can lead to emotional or physical problems later on.

In grieving you need to be aware of both your *thoughts* and your *feelings*. One widower came to us after reading one of our books, *Getting to the Other Side of Grief*, which deals with grief following the death of a spouse. He claimed that he had read the entire book and done all the exercises but still didn't feel any better. After asking a few questions, we learned that his wife had died only three months earlier and that he had approached his grieving like he did his job as an efficiency consultant to organizations! He had taken the totally cognitive, rational approach. He read the book, followed the suggestions, and thought he should be better. He didn't understand that he needed to deal with his feelings and that this process couldn't be rushed. Working through all of your feelings takes *time*, which is the other critical factor you need along with doing grief *work* in order to journey through grief.

There are three things to remember about the connection between your emotions and your grief. *First*, you need to realize that emotions are natural responses to all kinds of situations. We all have feelings. We don't have to justify them to others. They just exist. Remember how we said earlier that our emotions and thoughts often conflict with each other while we are grieving? This task of grief challenges you to be very intentional about differentiating between your thoughts and feelings. Thoughts can be debated, and you can argue with someone else to defend your thinking. While grieving, most of us don't really like to get into that. We just want what we say to be respected. That's why it is often preferable to tell people how you feel rather than what you think. So remember to identify and talk about your feelings.

Not only are emotions a natural response to your loss, but they are also healthy. We all have emotions that we may label as negative like sad and mad. But they are not wrong. They are neither good nor bad. They just *are*. Normally people associate the emotion of sadness with being a bad thing or something to quickly change. After all, we live in a culture that continually tells us we should be happy and not worry. So when people hear that sadness and anger are really normal feelings and that they don't need to flee from them but rather embrace and experience them, they are sometimes understandably reluctant to actually do that. However, you will undoubtedly have negative feelings while grieving, and learning how to deal with those feelings in a healthy way is a necessary thing to do.

Second, we believe that people need to decide how to respond to their emotions. We often use the image of a bottle to represent the receptacle where emotions go if they are internalized. If a person swallows feelings by not allowing for their expression, those feelings do not go away. Instead they are being stored. They accumulate in the bottle, and when the bottle gets too full, feelings can manifest themselves in a variety of undesirable ways, such as depression, anxiety, or a physical illness.

It is healthiest to be congruent in expressing your thoughts and, even more so, your feelings to those involved with your grief issues. The principle of congruence calls for honesty and integrity in assertively stating what you think and feel, and then behaving by your words and actions in ways consistent with your thoughts and feelings. So, be congruent by not pretending you are okay when you're not, especially when others ask how you're doing. It is healthiest to express emotions honestly rather than to tell people what you think they'd like to hear. Remember that if emotions are honestly and openly expressed and dealt with, you can eventually work through them, and they will dissipate as you let them go. Doing that may also make you more vulnerable to others, but in the process it draws you closer, and you can hopefully feel even more connected with them.

Third, feelings are so individual that you should not expect others to have or express them in the same way. So don't be afraid to be truly *you* in what and how you communicate. Your gender influences your emotional expression as well. Both men and women may experience some similar emotions of grief, but stereotypically they express their feelings differently. Men tend to be more closed, often trying to appear strong and in control because they have been taught that "real men" do not cry. Women, on the other hand, tend to be more openly expressive. Crying is more often expected and accepted in females, according to traditional societal norms. We would encourage you to recognize that combining traditionally masculine and feminine characteristics provides the healthiest approach to grieving for both men and women. So give appropriate expression to your emotions based on your own unique personality, gender, and culture so the emotions won't accumulate and eventually cause damage. One of the most prevalent reasons why a person might get stuck on the grief detour is that their emotional receptacle is overflowing with swallowed or suppressed feelings. Don't let that happen to you. Honestly express your feelings so they can get out!

Specific Ways to Work on Your Grief

✚ Recognize that all the feelings associated with the death of your loved one, such as anger, guilt, sadness, remorse, and relief, are normal. Grieving people are often embarrassed to openly express their feelings because they fear others will think they are "losing it." If you are grieving, you might even think that you're going crazy. Be assured that any feeling is okay unless you are feeling actively suicidal; that is, if you have a plan and intend to act on it. If that is the case, you need to contact your doctor or grief therapist, or go to the emergency room to get immediate help.

✚ Be "real" rather than trying to cover up your feelings. Don't pretend. Expressing emotions is a healthy thing to do. Find a supportive person who is a caring listener. Emotions and tears are a normal part of grieving, so don't worry about what other people will think or may want from you. When asked, for example, "How are you doing?" have the courage to say something like, "It is such a struggle for me to live without [name]" or "I'm feeling sad so much of the time." By doing this you are being congruent.

✚ Purchase a journal and write in it on a regular basis to record your thoughts and feelings in one place. Write down what you think and feel about what is happening. Write something like "I feel [name of feeling] about [whatever it is] because [the reason, if you know what it is]." Remember, your writing doesn't have to be grammatically correct. No one else will read it. But journaling helps you validate your feelings, identify and sort through what you think and feel, guide some of your necessary grief work, recall what you have already worked through so you can see your progress when you read earlier entries, and do some important problem solving. Journaling will also help you understand that all your feelings are legitimate—not right or wrong—and that they will probably decrease or change over time and will eventually become only a memory.

✚ Letter writing is another form of journaling that provides an excellent emotional outlet whether you intend to send the letter or not. You can write directly to the deceased or to others who were involved with the deceased, such as medical personnel, a spiritual caregiver, the funeral director, or your relatives, to express your thoughts and feelings to them. You will gain more self-awareness by doing this, and you will deepen your understanding of your grief. This activity can help dissipate and neutralize your negative feelings. We recommend you write a letter to your deceased loved one on all the significant days (such as holidays, the deceased's birthday, the anniversary of the death, and so on). Then go to the cemetery or a special location to read it out loud.

✚ Put yourself in situations that may trigger grief even though this may be painful. This is "doing the tough stuff." Grieving people are often afraid of doing things that might make them cry, particularly around other people. Yet, if you do not eventually face these things, you will prolong your grief. Giving power to a situation, place, or activity because you are afraid to face it allows that thing to have a degree of control over your life. Remember, being easy on yourself is a form of avoidance. Give yourself permission to back off at times, but not for the long term. When you have a spurt of energy, grasp the opportunity to face something that will be emotionally challenging. Plan specific times to do something related to your loved one that will make you cry. Crying will help you get out feelings and feel better.

✚ If you are still planning the funeral events, know that the funeral process can both allow for and elicit feelings in ways that are beneficial for you. Separating the funeral events, as we discussed before, gives you an opportunity to emotionally absorb the reality of the death and express your feelings. If the funeral has already occurred, replay the events in your mind, or look at funeral mementoes and journal your experiences as a way to further release your emotions.

✚ Carefully consider the use of medications (antidepressants, anti-anxiety agents, or sleeping aids) to help you deal with your grief. The attitude that society has to make it "easier" on everyone is actually counterproductive to getting through grief. Sometimes society behaves as though a person just needs to take a pill to fix things. That certainly isn't the case with grief. The more alert and aware you can be throughout the entire grief process, the more helpful it will be for your grief journey. Of course, even without the use of medications, usually a layer of numbness will initially protect you from an emotional intensity greater than you can tolerate. However, if after a month or so following the death you still have difficulty getting a minimum of five hours of sleep a night or getting out of bed in the morning, or have to exert a great deal of effort to perform daily tasks of living or go to work as needed, an anti-depressant may be necessary to help you function better. Medications don't give anyone permission to avoid dealing with grief. They cannot take the place of grief work or blot out your feelings. But some people do need the help of medications to initially give them the motivation to work through the grief tasks. Medications are definitely necessary if you are feeling actively suicidal. If you have any questions about your own use of medications while grieving, we encourage you to consult your physician and grief therapist (if you are in therapy).

✚ Use pictures, videos, and stories of the funeral events and of your prior relationship with the deceased to express your emotions. Reviewing pictures, mementoes, cards, letters, and the like can help trigger your feelings during your entire grief process. Remember that eliciting these feelings helps empty the receptacle, which ultimately contributes to healing the pain of grief.

✚ Attend a grief support program at your funeral home or one sponsored by another agency or faith community in your area. Many cities have chapters of AARP's Grief and Loss programs (including services for those widowed), Compassionate Friends for child loss, THEOS programs (To Help Each Other Spiritually), and bereavement support groups and workshops sponsored by hospice organizations, all to help you cope with your loss. Local hospitals, churches, and synagogues in your vicinity may also offer grief support services. If you are not aware of the resources available in your area, check with your funeral director or a leader in your faith community.

THE SPIRITUAL PERSPECTIVE

Where Are You, God?

> *Job 2:4–6: "Skin for skin!" Satan replied. "A man will give all he has for his own life. But now stretch out your hand and strike his flesh and bones,*

*and he will surely curse you to your face." The
LORD said to Satan, "Very well, then, he is in your
hands; but you must spare his life."*

Job 19:7-11: *"Though I cry, 'Violence!' I get no
response; though I call for help, there is no justice.
He has blocked my way so I cannot pass; he has
shrouded my paths in darkness. He has stripped
me of my honor and removed the crown from
my head. He tears me down on every side till
I am gone; he uproots my hope like a tree. His
anger burns against me; he counts me among his
enemies."*

- **May I be upset with God? How do I manage my
  feeling of being abandoned by God in my moment
  of greatest need?**

You may be feeling isolated and alone right now. No
one else knows just how lonely and hurting you are.
You may think you have been abandoned, as though
no one cares. Your relationship with God may be a big
disappointment. You may have thought that because
God loves you, and you are a believer, he would protect
you against bad things in life. The death of a loved one
is definitely one of the most hurtful things you will ever
have to endure. Perhaps you just want to yell at God
or pummel on his chest right now, and ask what he

possibly could have been thinking to allow the death of this special person in your life.

Job would understand your anger at God and your questioning why he allowed this awful thing to occur. You may be helped by reading the entire book of Job to understand the depths of Job's despair. He questions God about where he is and why God doesn't let him die too. Maybe you have felt like that at times. You might think that you would be better off dead along with your loved one rather than having to move forward.

As a result of your sense of abandonment and extreme disappointment in God, you may not want to talk with God or worship him. This is a normal reaction when a person feels so hurt by another. The tendency to withdraw from the offending person is quite common. Those feelings need to be expressed to God. Write him a letter. Journal about how upset you are. Get it all out. Ask him to help you understand this pain of your loved one's death.

Look further at the case of Job. God hadn't left him. True, he didn't relieve Job of his pain, but he was there all the time. Job just wasn't aware of God's hand holding him up until the trauma had ended. Isn't that also true of us? Sometimes it is difficult in the middle of intense strife to see God working within and through us. Hopefully as you make progress on your detour, you can have a little better perspective on your grieving. Perhaps you will then be able to see God's hand using evil (like death) to weave some threads of blessings into the mix. God has been with you all the time, holding you up, even when you're upset with him, because he really does love you. Job 42:12 says, "The LORD blessed the latter part of Job's life more than the former part." That may be difficult to believe, but it can actually happen in your life too.

Remember, God didn't want this pain for Job from the beginning. It was Satan, the evil one, who boasted that he could get Job to curse God if Job didn't have it so good. So God *allowed* Satan to bring all these calamities to Job's life, including the death of his beloved family. Remember, God didn't want death for us either. He has other blessings in store for you yet. In his love he orchestrated a final plan where after death comes the best of all—eternal life with him in Christ. Believe that with all your mind and heart. But also remember in the meantime that God is with you—right now and for always. Count on it.

Prayer: Dear Lord, King of the universe, I am mystified by the drama you engaged in with Satan and Job. Help me see clearly that you were and still are all-powerful and in ultimate control. Help me believe that you will never abandon me. Even now, in my grief, assure me of your presence and your blessing. *Amen*

Tears in the Night

> ***Romans 8:22–23:*** *"We know that the whole creation has been groaning as in the pains of childbirth right up to the present time. Not only so, but we ourselves, who have the firstfruits of the Spirit, groan inwardly as we wait eagerly for our adoption, the redemption of our bodies."*
>
> ***John 11:35:*** *"Jesus wept."*

- **Why is it important to be sad and cry rather than just focus on the joy and victory of the Christian life? What if I can't pray or go to church right now?**

Have you had well-meaning friends tell you that God works all things for good and won't give you more than you can handle? They may suggest you need to rejoice in all things and focus on your victory in Christ. If you have heard these types of comments, you probably didn't find them very comforting or helpful, even if you do believe deep down that they are true. When death strikes and it seems like your world is crashing down, these platitudes don't offer much comfort, at least not during the early days of grieving. These messages all seem to say, "Cheer up, everything is going to be okay, so don't grieve."

First Thessalonians 4:13 clearly teaches that believers will grieve, but not as those who have no hope. God expects us to grieve. Grieving means expressing your feelings. Jesus did. When he saw Lazarus dead, he wept. Although Jesus knew that in just a short time he would raise Lazarus from the dead, he still expressed his deep sadness through tears. Being created in God's image, we also have emotions, a quality that separates us from all other creatures. We not only need to accept that we are created as emotional beings, but also we need to express these emotions openly. The Bible never downplays emotions. It embraces feelings that are both positive and negative. You may like the passages that talk about joy in the Lord and celebrate his greatness. But the Bible also embraces the other end of the emotional continuum. The entire universe groans and cries aloud with pain waiting for the final redemption in Christ (Rom. 8:22–23). Life isn't all joy, peace, and happiness. We only know what joy is when we understand its counterpart of sorrow. Sometimes joy and sorrow exist together in an intriguing blend of feelings, but many times we just experience the intense pain, sadness, and longing of grief.

Perhaps right now you don't want to go to church because it is too difficult or too emotional. Maybe you hurt so much that no one wants to venture near you when you're filled with such pain. Or maybe you don't want to face others and have to answer their routine question, "How are you?" without telling them the truth through your tears. The worship service may elicit a myriad of feelings. The songs. The place. The memories. The message touches a nerve. It's painful. The dam breaks, and a flood of tears bursts out. Self-consciously you exit the church midservice and decide you can't go back for a while.

We hope you know all of this is perfectly normal for those who are grieving. Eventually, whether you stay away from church for a while, worship privately, or decide to sit in the back of the church and cry softly and then leave, you will gradually experience less difficulty worshiping through an entire service. God understands and puts his arms around you. He has promised to turn your mourning into dancing and clothe you with joy (Ps. 30:11). So cry those tears when they come in the night, in church, or in the morning, assured that God's arms are around you and that he will help you walk through this valley.

Prayer: God of all compassion, I know you understand my tears. Please hear the cries of my heart. Let me cry to you because you have promised that you will be there when I am hurting and feeling sad. Even in my confusion and my fear, help me trust that you are the answer to my pain. Assure me that my weeping will last only a little while longer, and that you will provide a new dawning of your grace in my life. *Amen*

My Fist in the Face of God

> **Job 3:1–4:** "After this, Job opened his mouth and
> cursed the day of his birth. He said: 'May the day
> of my birth perish, and the night that said, "A boy
> is conceived!" That day—may it turn to darkness;
> may God above not care about it; may no light
> shine on it.'"

> **Job 30:20–23:** "I cry out to you, God, but you do
> not answer; I stand up, but you merely look at
> me. You turn on me ruthlessly; with the might of
> your hand you attack me. You snatch me up and
> drive me before the wind; you toss me about in the
> storm. I know you will bring me down to death, to
> the place appointed for all the living."

• **Is being angry and arguing with God a bad thing?
What does it mean to "lament"? If Jesus lamented
and wept, may I do that too?**

Job is certainly waving his fist in the face of God.
You can almost see him prancing around with his fists
clenched in front of him like a boxer taunting God, "Go
ahead, God. Hit me again. Hit me till I fall. Bring me
all the way down—even to death itself." How does Job
dare say those things? After all, doesn't he remember
that God is his Creator, the one who has protected and
blessed him? Now, in the course of a little more than

a week, Job has it out with God in a full-fledged war of words.

Maybe Job's behavior isn't that strange. When someone you loved dearly dies, you may feel that God has not only abandoned you but also is intentionally trying to make things worse for you. You are numb with grief. Your friends don't know what to say (just like Job's friends). No one, it seems, is there to comfort you. Even God seems to have turned into your enemy. Like Job, you may curse the very day you were born. With Job you cry out, "You turn on me ruthlessly" (Job 30:21).

What is really going on here? First, remember that Job is not talking theologically but emotionally. These are cries of the heart. This is lament. Lament includes the all-out expression of our emotions—wailing and crying before God. Lament also challenges God to keep his promises. It is arguing with God. Tevye, in *The Fiddler on the Roof*, used a mild form of lament when he turned his face toward heaven and cried out, "Why couldn't you have made me a rich man? How would that have changed your eternal plan?" Your lament of grief is even greater and more serious than that. In your lament you wrestle with God. You cry out, "Why, O God, why?" You challenge him to keep his promises. How can things possibly work for your good?

But is it God's will that we suffer? Is it God's desire that we be overwhelmed in our grief? Absolutely not. This is all a result of sin and evil in our world. He may *allow* it for a little while, but finally, in Christ, we are victors! Job actually speaks with two voices. One voice is an emotional lament, cursing the day of his birth and accusing God of attacking him. But then Job speaks with the other voice—the voice of faith:

> I know that my redeemer lives, and that in the end he will stand on the earth. And after my skin has been destroyed, yet in my flesh I will see God; I myself will see him with my own eyes—I, and not another. How my heart yearns within me!

> Job 19:25–27

Tonight is a night for tears, for lament. Lament is the all-out expression of anger, frustration, and fear to the Lord. It is calling on God to keep his promises during a time when he seems so distant from you. The night of grief is deep and dark. God may seem to be far away, or he may seem to be attacking you. Your tears may obliterate your view of God, just as rain obscures the view from a windshield. But God, the powerful Creator and Redeemer, is still there. His hand is outstretched. Your clenched fist needs to relax and grasp his hand, for he will lead you on toward a new day.

Prayer: You are the almighty God, greater than any power in this universe. Yet I want to wail in your presence, for sometimes you seem so very far away. I am so angry. My heart is broken with grief. I don't understand why you let this happen to me. Give me the ability to lament fully and still have the faith that when it is all done, I shall see you face to face. You are my redeemer. *Amen*

Four

Saying Good-Bye to the Old Road

THE MENTAL HEALTH PERSPECTIVE

Realistically Summarizing Your Life with the Deceased and Storing the Memories

Memories are reminders of the past that live on in our minds and hearts. They represent that portion of life that is now past. You undoubtedly have already stored many memories of your deceased loved one from your life together. They now reside in your memory and can be recalled at will. You move on, *and* you remember.

The third task on the grief journey is to *find a place for memories of the person who died that honors what you had together and acknowledges who you are now because of your relationship, but also makes room for you to move on.* This task will help you further understand and implement task one by accepting the "historical" aspect of your relationship with the deceased, and it adds an entirely new dimension to the grief journey. That is to say, whatever relationship you may have had with that person has now ended. It is in the past. It will never come back, but it has given you the gift of memories.

How do we create memories? Memories begin with the actual events or experiences we have by ourselves or with others. When the actual event is over, we have collected all kinds of information, feelings, and associations that are now stored in our minds—in our memories. These memories can be "awakened" either by our intentional recall of the event or by some other trigger like hearing a song or seeing a picture that brings the memory into our awareness. Memories are important to us because they are evidence of what our lives consisted of. They are the story of the life we lived with our loved ones.

Memories don't just "happen" to us. While we subconsciously store memories, we can also be very intentional about creating memories. We "memorize" things. So one of the biggest emotional challenges you face on your grief detour is taking the relationship you had with your loved one and now translating it all into memories.

Reviewing everything, including possessions of the deceased and places you went with the person, will assist you in this process. Doing this refreshes your memories for easy retrieval. What is especially challenging for many people is the mistaken notion that if they accept the reality of the death and begin to put this person in the past, somehow the memories of that person will fade. They think they will forget their loved one. Of course, that is not the case any more than we would forget any of the other important people and events in our lives. But here is another example of how emotions can often rule over the mind. We can become so afraid that we will forget that we actually believe it will happen, even though our minds tell us that this will not be the case.

Not all memories are pleasant, so what do you do with the unpleasant ones you might have of your loved one? You may actually want to forget some aspects of your relationship with the person who died, or you might think you will be disloyal to a person who isn't here to defend himself or herself if you say or think something negative about that person. We all realize that no one is perfect. Our personalities are a composite of everything we are—the good and the not-so-good. So remember this person realistically—the good and the bad together. If you don't do that, you will put that person on a pedestal and make moving through your grief that much harder or even impossible.

The difficulty of moving the deceased to the past and storing memories of him or her is that you need to say good-bye and let go of that person. Your loved one is no longer a part of your present life, and you won't be able to move on if you're still holding on to someone who now really belongs in your past. Saying good-bye and letting go doesn't mean that the relationship was not important to you. It has nothing to do with how much you loved the person. People who had healthy and happy relationships often have less difficulty letting go after honestly and heartily grieving than those with conflicted relationships. So begin to find ways to say good-bye again and again until you can truly move that person to your past, and he or she becomes a series of treasured memories that you can easily recall.

There is one other primary way your loved one can stay close to you in addition to your collection of memories of him or her. You are likely a different person in some specific ways because of how this person impacted your life. He or she may have deeply influenced your beliefs, your values, your religious faith, your habits and customs, and your lifestyle. Perhaps you enjoy certain activities partially because this person had introduced you to them. You may find yourself reflecting on how your loved one influenced and changed your life. You may hear yourself saying, "I wouldn't be doing this or be involved in that if it weren't for [name]!" So in addition to your memories, you now have a life perspective and a lifestyle that has been deeply affected because he or she was a part of your life. Who you are now includes those influences of all the people who have been close to you, for they have in some sense become a part of you, and you take all of that with you throughout your life.

Specific Ways to Work on Your Grief

✚ Over time, if you are the person closest to the deceased, go through all your loved one's possessions, remembering how the person looked and behaved and the times you had together. Recall their love for various activities or interests. When you look through your loved one's clothing and all the other things he or she acquired, you will be cementing your memories of that person. You will begin to put that person in your past, realizing that your loved one will never use the clothes or all the other possessions again. There may be some items you wish to keep in a memory box to look at from time to time or on special occasions to remember the deceased person. Some of these may be items you want to keep until the time seems right to give them to another family member as a special keepsake. You now face the need to accept the reality that your loved one isn't coming back, and in doing so you will continue the process of letting go.

✚ Review and edit all the pictures, videos, slides, and other memorabilia. Make a picture book, scrapbook, or memory book of the life you and your deceased loved one had together. Put it where you can look at it frequently to recall your memories.

✚ Summarize your loved one's life realistically; don't "sanitize" their memory. Think and speak about your loved one accurately in both positive and negative ways. Eventually be able to identify not only all the positives but some of the things that you do not miss about the deceased, such as now you don't have to go to a restaurant you didn't care for, or watch science fiction movies when you prefer comedies.

✚ Put your relationship with the deceased on a lifeline. Actually draw a line (maybe you'll need to tape pages together) and plot your birth date and other significant points in your life on that line. Include the beginning of your relationship with the deceased as well as their death to see where it began and where it now ends.

Mark and label all the other significant times you had with your loved one. Your life needs to move on, so make sure your line extends beyond the point of your loved one's death. You have more things to experience and accomplish in this world even if right now you have no idea what those things might be.

✚ Write a story of your relationship with the deceased from its beginning to the time of their death. Include in that story such things as your predominant memories, what you valued most and least about the relationship, and how your life has been affected because of your relationship together.

✚ Identify and incorporate ways your deceased loved one enhanced your life, and how you are different because you were their spouse, child, parent, sibling, or friend. In other words, as you move through your grief journey you will be able to determine how you grew because of your relationship with that person.

✚ Visit places that were special in your relationship together, such as restaurants, vacation spots, parks, or beaches. Remember the times you spent together there. Do many of the same things that were special to the two of you or your family *without* the person who died. This is often a very difficult and emotional experience, but so very important. It helps you recall events, disempowers the place somewhat each time you revisit it, and helps you decide if you still like it without your deceased loved one. When you go to these special places or are with people who were significant to you and your loved one, be aware of the empty place previously occupied by your loved one. That will help you remember, relive events, and then decide if you still want to do that activity or be with those people without your deceased loved one.

✚ Celebrate the positive aspects of your loved one's life by listening to the tape of the tributes friends and family had given at the funeral. Reread comments or stories that people had written about your loved one, and read things you may have written yourself about him or her. You might ask family and friends to write down their favorite stories or ways they appreciated this person so you can put them in a memory book to help honor and remember the person who died.

✚ Use the past tense as much as possible to refer to the deceased. That means "was" rather than "is," because the relationship no longer has a present or a future. If your child died, talk about things that belong*ed* (past tense) to your child while she or he was alive. Your loved one is no longer living and physically present.

✚ Use any religious, cultural, or family ritual that emphasizes the transition of the relationship from a present reality to an honored memory. This may be a candle-lighting ceremony, a toast, the singing of a favorite song, reading a special story or Scripture passage, making the person's favorite food, or participating in a memorial event, but especially emphasize the "we remember" and "in the past" aspects of the ritual.

➕ Recognize there will be many ways and times you will need to say good-bye to your loved one before you have completed the detour of grieving. Write in a letter to your deceased loved one on special occasions how you feel about the prospect of spending the day without him or her. You can write things like, "You will never be here again to celebrate Christmas with me. I hate that thought, but I need to say good-bye to our Christmas times together."

➕ Give a gift to a charity or special cause in memory of your loved one. This becomes a tangible way to memorialize the person and benefit a special interest he or she had.

➕ Be cautious about using websites that invite people to post messages to deceased loved ones as if active communication were still possible. Real communication involves two physically present people who can exchange thoughts and feelings together. We discourage any type of Internet connection that suggests the possibility that your deceased loved one can actually receive or respond to correspondence you may send.

However, we certainly encourage writing journal letters to the deceased as a therapeutic expression.

✚ Know that you will *never* forget your loved one, but you will eventually remember that person free from the pain of your grief. When you are no longer in pain, that will be one of several signals that you probably have come to the end of your grief detour and have finished your grieving.

THE SPIRITUAL PERSPECTIVE

Memories

> *Luke 22:17–19: "After taking the cup, he [Jesus] gave thanks and said, 'Take this and divide it among you. For I tell you I will not drink again of the fruit of the vine until the kingdom of God comes.' And he took bread, gave thanks and broke it, and gave it to them, saying, 'This is my body given for you; do this in remembrance of me.'"*

• **How does the Bible encourage us to create and use memories? How can I make meaning out of the death and cherish my memories of my loved one?**

The person you loved has died. The reality of the death is hard enough to accept and believe. As the shock and numbness begin to diminish, however, something else happens. Memories! An onslaught of images, sounds, smells—each one triggering reminders of both good and tough times. What do you do with the memories, especially when they seem to be both comforting and disturbing at the same time?

God wants you to remember even as you move on in your life. Memories do two things—one of which is often unpleasant, the other pleasant. The unpleasant part is that a memory marks the fact that you have moved on. In the passage quoted above, Jesus is eating the last earthly meal with his disciples prior to his death. They sense the danger that lies ahead of them. Judas has already been revealed as the one who would betray Christ. Then Jesus does a strange thing. He talks about the wine as his blood and bread as his body. He instructs his disciples to repeat this sacrament "in remembrance of me" (Luke 22:19). Something tangible, like bread and wine, is now to serve as a lasting memorial of Christ's life, death, and eventual resurrection. The tough part is knowing the actual event can't be repeated. Jesus's meal with his disciples was the actual event. The sacrament of the Lord's Supper becomes the memorial. You *had* a special relationship with your loved one. But with their death, that relationship has become a memory—a thing from the past—part of your history. That's the hard part.

The pleasant part is that God embraces and encourages memories. So churches and believers repeat the sacrament of the Lord's Supper regularly. In this sacrament, believers remember both the pain Christ endured on the cross because of our sin and the joy of his resurrection for our salvation on Easter morning. God wants you to keep significant memories alive and fresh. At first, the memories of your loved one may be painful. They may awaken a deep yearning within you to have that special person back in your life. But as you move through your grief, these memories will bring comfort, assurance, a smile to your face, and a warm glow around your heart.

There is one other thing about Christian memories suggested by Christ's memorial sacrament. Surely, the bread and wine were chosen to help us remember the events of his death and resurrection. But they also encourage us to remember God's role in this. Of all the memorials in the Bible, this is the one that most directly reminds us that life does come after death!

God sees the big picture. Hopefully in time you will be able to see the big picture as well. Collect your memories. Go ahead and remember your loved one fully and honestly. In remembering, focus not only on your deceased loved one but also on the loving and saving hand of God in your grief and for eternity.

Prayer: Dear Lord, I know that you ask me to remember your great power. Help me understand that some day, hopefully soon, I can look back on my grief and see your powerful hand leading and guiding me. Help me remember my loved one completely and honestly, and remember your grace and strength while I journey through grief. *Amen*

Must I Say Good-Bye Forever?

Matthew 22:30: *"At the resurrection people will neither marry nor be given in marriage; they will be like the angels in heaven."*

- **Will I recognize my loved one in heaven? Will I still be related to him or her? What does the Bible say (and not say) about human relationships in heaven?**

So many questions, and so few answers! The person you loved has died. Now you have the memories—only the memories! The questions begin to flood over you. Will I see her again? Will I know him when I get to heaven? Will she still be my grandmother in eternity? What age will he be? Will my baby who died still be a baby? Will I still have that very special intimate relationship with my spouse? So many questions, and the Bible, quite honestly, does not address most of them.

The Gospels of Matthew, Mark, and Luke all tell the story of the Sadducees (who didn't believe anyone could be raised from the dead) trying to trip up Jesus. "A man dies," they said, "and his brother marries his widow" (which was the cultural practice in the days of Jesus). Then this second brother dies, and so the next brother marries her—and so on, until she has married all seven brothers, and the seventh finally dies. "So now," the Sadducees ask, "if there really is a resurrection, whose wife will she be?" (see Matt. 22:23–33). They assumed that she would have to be married to one of them—the first or the last, or anyone in between. If that were so, resurrection would cause a real problem because she might have seven husbands! So in their thinking, resurrection is not an option. We marry. We die. We are buried. And it's over.

But Jesus challenges that idea by not addressing the issue of resurrection but rather the issue of marriage. "She won't be married at all," he replied. "There is no marriage in heaven." Now that is terribly sad news, especially if your husband or wife has died. This raises all kinds of questions. What will our relationship be with the family and friends we had on this earth?

Let's look at it this way. On this earth, family relationships are defined by bloodlines or legal decrees. The state declares us to be married or to have legally adopted a child. By bloodlines you are related to brothers and sisters, parents and grandparents, and your children.

But in heaven, Jesus says, we will all be like the angels. That doesn't mean we will sprout wings and play harps. We think this means two things. First, angels don't die; and second, they are not sexual beings. There is no need for them to procreate and to replenish the earth. That doesn't mean that all the other aspects of a marriage are of no importance—the kinship, the love, the dreams and goals. These are still very important. But like everything else in heaven, our relationships will be redefined.

As students of the Bible, we have beliefs about what it will be like in heaven, and we hope you find these helpful and comforting. First, we think we will still recognize each other because we will retain aspects of our personal identity and personality. Second, we will not be concerned about the way we related to each other on this earth. Our former relationships will be overshadowed by being part of God's greater family once we are in heaven. Our family on earth was defined through our parents. Our family in heaven will be defined by our relationship with God our Father, Jesus the Son, and all of us as God's adopted children (Eph. 1:5). Everything we thought was wonderful, satisfying, and valuable about our relationships on earth will be superseded by the fantastic relationship we will have with Christ our Savior. Heaven will be, after all, truly Paradise!

Prayer: Dear Lord, while I deeply yearn to see my loved one again, I know that I too want to experience your heavenly home when I die. Help me not only believe in the final resurrection but also rise to the challenge of living my life right now to its fullest extent. Give me the strength to face each new day. *Amen*

The Road Ahead Looks Scary

Jeremiah 29:11: *"For I know the plans I have for you," declares the* Lord, *"plans to prosper you and not to harm you, plans to give you hope and a future."*

Hebrews 12:1–2: *"And let us run with perseverance the race marked out for us, fixing our eyes on Jesus, the pioneer and perfecter of faith. For the joy set before him he endured the cross,* *scorning its shame, and sat down at the right hand of the throne of God."*

- **Do I have purposes beyond what I had with my loved one? How do I determine what those purposes in life are now?**

One of the most powerful feelings that often rolls over the heart of someone who is grieving is the feeling of drifting aimlessly, neither knowing nor caring about what they will do next. When pressed about this, many will say something like, "Now that [name] has died, I really don't have a reason to go on. All my dreams and my future died when my loved one died." If the feeling isn't quite that strong, a grieving person might still say something like, "I really have no idea what I'm going to do now. I don't have a sense of direction for my life."

God created us to have a direction and purposes for our life. For careers we call it a vocation. In relationships, we call it intimacy. In our walk with God, we call it growing up in the Lord. In our leisure and recreation, we call it a sense of fulfillment or enjoyment. But we do things and love people because they help fulfill a sense of purpose on our life journey.

Grief aborts that sense of direction, and in our grief we need to hear words like those from Jeremiah 29. On the brink of going into captivity again, Israel needed to know that this wasn't the end of it all. They still had a future, a hope. That future and hope rested in the hands of God himself. They may have been depressed. They may have felt like they were going to wander aimlessly again through the wilderness. But God said clearly that he hadn't forgotten them. Just like he had for Israel, God has plans for you—"plans to give you hope and a future" (Jer. 29:11).

There is something uncomfortable, though, about this passage in Jeremiah. God's plan was *not* to rescue the Israelites from their imminent defeat and impending captivity. They would have to experience all of that. Actually, God said that it would last seventy years. But nevertheless, God still had plans for them. Even though you presently have to face some really tough times in your grief, God wants you to know that he still has plans that go way beyond what you are facing right now.

Jesus is the primary example of knowing that God had a plan, but a plan that first of all involved pain and suffering for him as our savior. He, however, could see beyond the cross to the "joy set before him" (Heb. 12:2).

You may not be able to see the future as clearly as Jesus could. Actually, you probably can't imagine what your future will look like at all. In that case, learn from the examples of Jeremiah and Jesus. Trials, challenges, and grief do come our way. But God takes this trouble up into his plan and brings us well beyond it. God can take all this pain and suffering, and through his grace and power, turn it to our "profit" (Heb. 12:10–11).

This is not meant to minimize the grief and pain you feel. On the contrary, the Bible says that it is okay to feel and express that pain, being confident that God is there holding your hand and leading you on, saying, "Follow me, I have a plan for your life."

Prayer: My life seems to have no direction, yet you tell me that you have plans and purposes for me, Father. Let me know the reasons for my being here. My loved one has died, but I know that I haven't died. Reveal to me what you want me to do now. I rest in your directing power. *Amen*

Five

Setting My Sights on a New Direction

THE MENTAL HEALTH PERSPECTIVE

Getting to Know Who You Are Now

Simply stated, the fourth task of grief is to *adjust to life by deciding who you are as an individual without your deceased loved one.* As a bereaved person, you need to recognize that your life is ultimately an individual journey. Your life may have been so closely linked to your deceased loved one that it is difficult to realize that you are your own unique person. It may feel like a part of you is missing. Now you must (re)define yourself after your loved one's death. This is particularly challenging for almost all bereaved people. For a bereaved spouse it means accepting that you are now alone without a partner, and yet you are still a whole, complete individual. Or, if you were a parent, you may no longer function as such following your child's death if you have no other children. Likewise, you will no longer be a child to anyone when both of your parents have died, or a sibling if you have no other living brothers or sisters. If you had one best friend, you no longer have that best friend. Death changes the roles we play, and those roles help define us.

Now you also need to reevaluate the various interests and activities you participated in because of, or with, the person who died. Will you continue to do those things (such as boating, attending the theater, helping out at school, or going to sports events) now that your loved one is no longer here to participate with you? You need to ask yourself, "Who was I before my deceased loved one came into the picture?" "Who was I *with* that loved one?" "Who am I now *without* that person in my life?" And eventually the question will become, "Who am I *now*?"

Figuring out who you are independent of your deceased loved one is a necessary part of getting through this grief detour. Other people might come alongside you to offer comfort and support, but you need to take charge of your life and figure out who you are now. The principle behind this task, regardless of what type of loss you have experienced, is quite simple but also very profound: we are all individual persons, whole and complete in and of ourselves. We don't *need* another person to make us whole or complete, even though we may *want* people around to enhance our lives. Certainly we grow together in our marriages, or we live in special relationships with our children, siblings, or parents. We all are social beings to some extent, although some like to be surrounded by people more than others. But we must recognize that by birth we are complete persons by ourselves and capable as adults of living without any one specific person in our lives.

This fourth task means you recognize that you have a life independent of the one you had with the deceased person. That person obviously impacted the contours of your life. But you now need to begin finding ways to reinvest in life on your own terms without that person. You will have to begin making decisions without considering the one who died. This fourth task, then, addresses the need for you to evaluate where you feel painfully empty because of your past connection with the deceased, determine how you want to fill that emptiness, and reconstruct your own identity without a relationship with that person. You have to work at knowing and loving yourself, discovering and engaging in your own interests and activities, developing a renewed caring for others, and determining your own life purposes now.

Specific Ways to Work on Your Grief

✚ Write down and analyze what roles you will and will no longer play following the death of your loved one. Draw a circle and section off all the roles you play in your life, including those you had with your deceased loved one. Cut the circle like a pie into pieces the size of the role investment you made, for example, as a spouse, parent, adult child, sibling, co-worker, friend, and with yourself. This will help you see how much time and energy you devoted to each relationship and how big a space the deceased person occupied in your life—this is the primary area that now needs reconstruction and development.

✚ After you recognize what roles your deceased loved one played in your life, you will have to determine how you will compensate for that loss. Listing the roles or writing them in a letter to your deceased loved one may be very helpful, saying, for example, "These are all the ways you contributed to my life to my benefit. Thank you so much, but now I have to determine how to manage these things without you." Then begin to explore ways to fill the voids.

✚ Identify your own personal interests and activities and how they compare with those of the person who died. You will no longer need to consider their interests in making your plans. Now you can personally decide if you want to pursue any of those things your deceased loved one enjoyed. Feeling compelled to continue something only out of a sense of loyalty is not healthy or helpful.

✚ Recognize that you are an important person whose thoughts, feelings, and ideas really do matter. Revisit the hopes and dreams you had before this person was in your life. Look at who you are becoming as you learn more about yourself on this grief detour. Grieving is a growth process in which you become more aware of what is important and gain a clearer sense of direction and purpose. This means that changes are occurring. Don't allow people to pressure you back into an old mold. Take a break from some of your prior activities to explore other options you have. Try new things before deciding what you like and want in your life *now*.

✚ Analyze other social and family relationships and decide which ones you want to maintain or enhance. Each individual relationship requires time for it. Following the death of your loved one, you now have the time that relationship took available for other things. However, you also have to compensate for all the things your loved one did, especially if he or she lived with you. Eventually you will probably want to invest in other and new relationships, but do not do this at the expense of your journey through the grief detour. We are talking mostly about friendships, but if you have been widowed and are considering dating, our strong recommendation is that you wait at least a year before beginning to date and also that you be certain you are finished grieving first. A person needs to feel single and whole again and accept the fact that the relationship with the deceased is over before moving into another romantic relationship. Remember that it takes time and energy to work on the tasks of grieving. Make that your first priority before pursuing other arenas.

✚ Recognize that insecurity and a lack of confidence are normal when you try to determine who you are right now. Part of your self-confidence may have been fueled by the support you received from the person who died. Without that validation, a sense of personal inadequacy and a lower level of self-esteem can creep in. Make encouraging comments to yourself about your own qualities, abilities, and worth. You are a good person. You do have many capabilities. Figure out who you are and be your own person.

✚ Know that you can wait a while to select a gravestone. Your funeral director can put a temporary marker at the grave site, so you can decide later about something permanent. Many surviving spouses tend to choose a double headstone at the time of death because of the closeness they experienced with their spouse. However, you may realize (especially if you are relatively young) that a decision made too early may be solely an emotional one. Choosing a dual headstone may sometimes conflict with a healthy separation from the deceased or detract from realizing that your life will eventually go on. Many people erroneously believe they will be reunited in the afterlife, and they want to try to maintain an unbroken connection with a deceased spouse through a shared headstone. We believe it is healthiest to realize your marriage is now over before making any decision regarding a headstone. Selecting a single headstone in no way eliminates the choice to someday be buried next to your deceased spouse.

✚ Realize that "getting back to normal" as soon as possible is *not* a healthy goal. Grieving takes time and work, and busyness is an avoidance or distraction to the process. You need to decide what suits you now. Give yourself the grief assignments that you have been reading about. Set specific time aside to do them. Revisit. Experience. Sort through. Journal. Rushing through the

---

process isn't helpful. Know that the "old" normal will never return—you must develop a "new" normal life pattern. The old pattern involved your deceased loved one who is no longer here. Now you need to develop your new life pattern—changed at least by the fact that you have one less person whom you love in your life.

✚ Realize that your life will go on. Even though you may feel awful right now, as though your life died with your loved one, trust that your life will improve with both the passing of time and your intentional grief work.

THE SPIRITUAL PERSPECTIVE

God Takes Care of Sparrows—and You

> **Matthew 6:26–27:** *"Look at the birds of the air; they do not sow or reap or store away in barns, and yet your heavenly Father feeds them. Are you not much more valuable than they?"*

• **Does my life still matter to God? What does it really mean that I am an individual creation of God? Why would God care about *me*?**

Are you not much more valuable than they? Are you? Sometimes in the middle of our grief, we think that no one else really cares. No one understands, and (more important) you don't either. You may get down on yourself. You may have to do things you've never done before and feel totally ill-equipped to do them. You may not have anyone guiding you, encouraging you, and building your confidence in what you are doing now or need to do next. *Worthless*, you think. *I really feel totally worthless!*

That is not an uncommon experience during grieving. Many times you may have depended on others to give you the affirmation and encouragement you needed. Or you may have felt good about having helped the person who had died but now wonder how you will go on without those responsibilities to give you a sense of purpose and worth in your life. When your loved one dies, you not only feel alone, but you can become terribly uncertain of yourself and lack the encouragement you need.

If this is happening to you, then it is time for a little self-talk as well as a talk with God. The self-talk hopefully comes rather naturally. You can likely hear yourself asking, "Who am I now that [name] has died? Do I still matter to anyone?" If you are raising questions about your self-esteem, tell yourself that you still do matter.

So then it's also time for a talk with God and to actually listen to what God has to say to you. The section of the Sermon on the Mount in Matthew 6:25–34 is frequently subtitled in many Bibles as "Don't Worry." The advice not to worry is based on one basic biblical truth—you are the most important part of God's entire creation. Jesus wasn't referring to all of us collectively, saying that human beings are more important than birds and flowers. He is saying that *you* personally are more important to him than anything else. So God's argument goes like this: if I take such good care of the birds and flowers, which are here one day and die the next, don't you think you are so much more valuable than they are?

We give gifts to people we love. A gift is an attempt to give visual evidence of the affection and appreciation we have for them. Hopefully in receiving a gift, you feel that value. How much more true is that for God? He gave *you* the magnificent gift of his Son, who died for your life. You are a treasure in his sight. You are always a very important person to God. Even as you say good-bye to your loved one, as you begin to store the memories of your life together, and as you begin to realize that you are on your own grief detour, know that your heavenly Father still sends this message: "I take care of the sparrows. I watch over the flowers of the field. Are *you* not much more valuable than they?"

Prayer: Take care of me, Father. You are so good to everything else you have created. I now need your special attention. Watch over me with the same tender care you give the sparrows. Please provide for my every need. Particularly help me be assured that you are watching over me and will give me a new sense of direction as I move through my grief. *Amen*

Letting Go . . . Letting God

1 Peter 5:7: *"Cast all your anxiety on him because he cares for you."*

Philippians 2:12–13: *"Therefore, my dear friends, as you have always obeyed—not only in my presence, but now much more in my absence—continue to work out your salvation with fear and trembling, for it is God who works in you to will and to act in order to fulfill his good purpose."*

• **If I trust and believe, won't God get me through this awful pain of grief? How does taking charge of my grief fit with putting it in God's hands? If I am widowed, does letting go mean removing my wedding ring?**

Letting go is very hard to do, like the toddler who doesn't dare let go of the furniture to take the first tentative steps. But letting go is necessary. The toddler can't enter adult life still hanging on to the furniture to get around.

The time comes on your grief journey when you too have to let go. But let go of what? Certainly, you will not let go of all your precious memories. You will not let go of the ways your life, values, and faith have been enhanced because of your relationship with this person. But you do finally have to let go and move that person from the present to the past tense. You now need to live each day being aware that he or she is not here, because that person has died and isn't coming back.

Even saying this directly may raise your anxiety level. The fear of forging ahead in life without your loved one can be intense. But God is the one who has plans for your life. These plans may very well involve many things you didn't originally think about. These plans may be greater and more fulfilling than you could even imagine. But letting go means redecorating and reusing your deceased child's room, or selling your parent's home. Letting go means redistributing everything your sibling had collected. Letting go means removing the wedding band from your marriage finger if your spouse died. Letting go—saying good-bye—is hard work. You will need to do it a thousand times, each time you let go of another tangible piece of your relationship with your loved one.

Don't overlook the "hard work" part of this equation. The issue isn't "*either* God will heal me *or* I have to work at it." The Bible says that our faith involves both God and us. In Philippians 2, Paul says that *we* have to work out our own salvation. This is our responsibility. We must believe. We must trust. We must obey. But then Paul immediately adds, "For it is God who works in you to will and to act in order to fulfill his good purpose" (Phil. 2:13). God is doing it too. You can apply this as well to your grief journey. You need to work at your grief, but you can do it with the confidence that God is simultaneously at work within you to heal your grief.

So when you engage in these difficult tasks of letting go, keep whispering quietly to yourself the words of 1 Peter 5:7: "Cast all your anxiety on him because he cares for you." Emphasize the last five words: "because he cares for you." He does care for you, especially as you let go of the past and prepare to enter your newly reconstructed life. Though you've been forced into a detour, you will get back on a main route again—hopefully by God's grace better for the experience, because God will guide and care for you in the process.

Prayer: You know, holy Father, the anxiety I have about so many things that are changing in my life. I tend to worry about big and little things. I am overwhelmed by everything that must be done—the decisions, the responsibilities, the expectations. Help me work through them, confident that you are working in me to get to the end of this grief detour. As I cast my anxieties on you, please take care of and guide me. *Amen*

Walking on Water

> *Matthew 14:28–32:* *"'Lord, if it's you,' Peter replied, 'tell me to come to you on the water.' 'Come,' he said. Then Peter got down out of the boat, walked on the water and came toward Jesus. But when he saw the wind, he was afraid and, beginning to sink, cried out, 'Lord, save me!' Immediately Jesus reached out his hand and caught him. 'You of little faith,' he said, 'why did you doubt?' And when they climbed into the boat, the wind died down."*

> *2 Corinthians 5:7:* *"We live by faith, not by sight."*

- **What does it mean to "live by faith, not by sight"? How can I discern God's will for my life now? If I become happy with life again, what will that say about my life with the deceased?**

Perhaps you are saying, "I'm not at all sure when this detour will end. How far down the road will I be when that happens? How will I get to my destination from here?" These are valid questions when you are on a detour, especially when detoured by grief. How do you get back on course once you have been rerouted? To continue to live fully doesn't sound possible while you are grieving, but as your pain and grief decrease, you may face a new confusion: "How do I figure out what I should do now? Where should I be—with my job, my family, my social group, my church community?"

When you do begin to move on, you may also wonder what people will think. Will they think that you are being disloyal? Or worse yet, will they think you really didn't like your life with your loved one that much anyway, because look at you now? Don't worry about what others think or say about your life now. Listen first to God, who still has plans for you.

The story in Matthew 14:28–32 talks about Jesus walking on the water. There he was, walking on top of the water to meet his disciples in their boat. No skis or motorboat pulling him. Then Peter asked Jesus if he could come to him, and he actually climbed out of the boat. No doubt on his part. But when he looked around, he became afraid. The waves were high, and he forgot that Jesus had said, "Come." His sinking faith caused him to sink as well. He needed Jesus to reach out and grab him. And Jesus did just that.

You may feel like you need to walk on water to put your life back in order. So much has changed in your life, and you may not know where to begin reconstructing it. But God also says to you, "Come, come with me. Walk where you never walked before. I, your Lord, can give you the confidence to begin taking a few steps." If you feel scared because you've never done this before, and you begin to sink, God will reach out and bolster you up. God is now asking you to move on without knowing where you are going. This is what the Bible means when it invites you to live by faith, not by sight. You probably can't understand very well how good can come out of the evil you experienced with the death of your loved one. Yet you are asked to trust and have faith. Even though you don't know the direction of the rest of your earthly journey, God does. He will reveal it one step at a time. He'll help you walk where you never walked before—even if it feels like you have to walk on water.

Prayer: Dear Lord, you have helped people do some amazing things. But what I am facing seems almost as impossible as walking on water. May I have the same confidence that Peter had at the beginning, the confidence to take the first steps into my reconstructed life. I may sink, just like Peter did. But I trust that you will continue to pick me up. Take me by the hand and lead me on, Lord. *Amen*

Six

Heading
for a Clear Road Ahead

THE MENTAL HEALTH PERSPECTIVE

Plotting a New Route for Your Journey

Just like wanting a detour to end, you are probably eager to be done grieving. Wouldn't it be nice to just snap your fingers and feel better, free from the pain of your loss and filled with enthusiasm for the future? Grieving, as you undoubtedly realize by now, doesn't work that way. But, just as with a detour, you aren't re-routed forever. Eventually you do get back to the main road. The route won't be exactly like it was before you were detoured by your grief. But the time will come when you are feeling better and are somewhat eagerly mapping out where you want to go when your detour finally comes to an end.

The fifth and final task of grief is to *reinvest fully in life*. As you separate your identity from that of your deceased loved one, you are setting the course for your journey as an individual without the person who died. Your life may look very different than it did before. The death of your loved one has changed a multitude of things. The old ways no longer fit because you must now do things without him or her. Obviously, the degree of change depends on the level of connection you had with the person who died. You may decide to continue heading in somewhat the same direction as before, but nevertheless your life will still look and feel different in some ways.

This final task is one of reinvesting in your "new normal" life as you reluctantly bid farewell to the "old normal." It may seem to you like standing on the deck of a cruise ship, waving good-bye to a loved one you will miss, but also being eager to discover what lies ahead of you on your trip. Because these tasks are not linear or sequential, reinvestment in life as an individual without your deceased loved one will happen in a number of little ways as you grieve. Relief and reassurance often come in small doses—each time you say or think, "I still like this" or "I can really do this on my own."

A primary goal of this task is to realize and accept that you have more life to live and to reinvest in it so that you do not become a "professional" griever. Research suggests that around 85 percent of bereaved people are able to establish a renewed life pattern without getting stuck in their grief. "Getting stuck" means not accepting the reality of your loss or emotionally letting go of your grief. You certainly will remember your grief (and, of course, the deceased person). You will even remember having the pain—but the pain itself will no longer be present. Moments may still come when sadness and perhaps a few tears briefly return, especially during major events or transitions such as marriages, graduations, other deaths, births of children or grandchildren, and the like. However, the pain likely will not be as intense or last as long as when you were grieving. You can get to the point where you can say that as far as you can determine you are done grieving, at least for now. We would then also encourage you to share that belief with others to help them understand you now are ready to move on.

You will have achieved a major goal when you have worked through your grief. Certainly, grieving has been difficult and painful. But your grief also ends. If you have worked on your grief, you have every reason to believe that within one to three years after your loved one's death (if there are no complicating factors), you will have healed and moved into a renewed vital life. While you will not be the same as you were before, many of the major features of your life will probably be similar. We often use the analogy of remodeling a house. Some renovations are relatively small and simple; others are more extensive. But in any case, you do not actually tear down the entire house and build a new one.

The grief journey involves some level of renovation. In many ways you are still the same person, but your life is not as it was previously because the place your loved one once occupied is now empty. You can't go back to yesterday. You are in the process of finding a new normal to your life—life without your loved one. And grief will change you in new and different ways. But you won't be worse for the wear, although it may feel like that for a while. You can now begin to see new possibilities not only for the present but also for your future.

Reinvesting fully in life is a continual process that focuses on the questions "Who am I now?" (from the fourth task) and "How do I want to live my life now that my loved one has died?" (from this fifth task). These two tasks imply a challenge as these questions begin to flow shortly after your loved one died and continue throughout your grief process. That is one reason why returning too quickly to your previous activities, involvements, commitments, social groups, and even full-time work (if financially you can initially take time off from work) is not really the most desirable thing to do.

We know that our society does not like to see people in pain. Other people may breathe a sigh of relief when they see you returning to some of what was once "normal" rather than being focused on grieving and working on the tasks of grief. But remember, *you* are in charge of your life, so do yourself a huge favor and give yourself the time to grieve. Grieving at the time your loved one dies is definitely healthier than waiting until some later time. You will still have to actively deal with your grief no matter how long you wait. Grief doesn't go away on its own. Be intentional about working on the tasks of grief. Only by attending to them will you be able to put your deceased loved one in your past and truly reinvest in life in a new, full, and complete way.

You Know You Are Done Grieving When You . . .

- can talk about your deceased loved one and recall special memories without crying or feeling significant pain.

- have removed all of his or her clothes and other personal belongings from closets and drawers and have claimed those spaces for your own use if that person had lived with you, have made decisions about disposing of or using these things, and perhaps have placed some keepsakes in a memory box to store.

- have no rooms or places that could constitute a shrine to your deceased loved one.

- have rearranged furniture and pictures the way you want them and now have only a few pictures on display of your deceased loved one.

- can look at pictures of your loved one and remember both the positives and negatives of that person and your relationship with him or her.

- can go out with the friends, couples, and families you went with before (if you still desire to do so) and feel good about yourself without your deceased loved one.

- have developed new relationships with other people, such as with some single individuals if you were widowed, or perhaps others who have experienced similar losses (such as the death of a child, parent, sibling, or friend).

- have revisited all your significant and memorable places without your loved one to remember and store those memories and to evaluate whether that is still a place you want to claim as your own.

- enjoy doing things your deceased loved one would not have participated in.
- no longer do things you didn't enjoy but had done with and for the deceased because he or she wanted to.
- have developed and are comfortable with your own decision-making process.
- are energized by your new or renewed sense of direction.
- can be by yourself and not feel lonely or yearn for your deceased loved one.
- have dealt with all the feelings (such as anger, guilt, remorse, regret, and sadness) that you may have felt about your relationship with the deceased.
- feel like you are a whole and complete person in yourself.
- can look in the mirror and smile at yourself and believe you will be all right.
- feel you have something to contribute to others.
- can recognize the positive aspects of being where you are in your life after grieving.

- know you are important and can be kind and caring to yourself by cooking nice meals, traveling, doing fun things, taking walks, and the like.
- believe you have completed the tasks of grief and have said good-bye for the last time.
- are satisfied and content with your life as it is now going.

In addition, if you were widowed, you also know you are done grieving when you:

- have removed your wedding ring from the fourth finger of your left hand and have decided what you will do with the ring.
- have devised a way to manage your sexuality appropriate to your value system.
- are comfortable checking the box "single" on forms and can embrace some of the advantages of being single.

Specific Ways to Work on Your Grief

✚ Work *through* your grief. Assess where you are at this point. Grief is not a dead-end street or a cul-de-sac. You *can* get to the other side and no longer feel the acute pain. You may have occasional moments of sadness, but the devastating pain of intense grief will eventually be gone. You can once again feel good about yourself and excited about your life.

➕ Make certain the pain is gone, and if not, identify what still triggers the pain. Review the activities and behaviors of the various tasks of grief that address your pain. Keep working on those areas until they no longer hurt. Hurting is a sign that you have not yet healed completely. Especially reread the section on desensitization in chapter 2 if you still experience pain in doing certain things. When doing something that is still painful, listen to what you are saying to yourself about that situation. Make certain you use positive self-talk, like, "I remember with joy doing this with [name], and I still like the activity, so I will find new ways to enjoy it now."

➕ As you go through the grief process, identify what will now be part of your "new normal" life pattern. What interests, activities, volunteer time, or work do you want to pursue? How is that the same or different than before your loved one died?

➕ Journal about what your loved one's death and your grieving process have taught you. Develop ways to live more fully through what you have learned and have become. Grieving will change you. You do grow through grief, that is, if you use it to help yourself grow. Perhaps you will appreciate the little things more or not get bent out of shape as easily when something goes wrong.

✚ Journal about what you now want to pursue. Make a list of your short- and long-term goals and develop a specific action plan beginning with small steps and eventually working toward bigger ones.

We hope you realize that although grief is a long and difficult detour on your life journey, you do not have to experience this grief for the rest of your life. Get a healthy start on grieving beginning with the funeral events and work on your grief consistently until you reach a satisfying finish. In assessing your progress, determine what you still need to do by referring to the lists of specific ways to work on your grief at the end of the mental health sections in the previous chapters, and use the preceding section on "You Know You Are Done Grieving When You . . ." as a final checklist. If you have followed these recommendations, no longer feel the pain of your loved one's death, and have gone through at least the first anniversary of the death (all four seasons), you may be ready to declare yourself to be finished grieving (as far as you can tell).

However, don't be discouraged if you think you still have a long way to go before being totally finished. Remember, grieving typically takes one to three years, and sometimes a little longer, before you are through the detour. Once you say, "Yes, I think I am through grieving!" then the healthy thing is to deliberately tell others your good news. Go "public" with your significant accomplishment. But do remember that coming to the end of your grief detour requires both an emotional readiness and a willful resolve to be done grieving and to move into your new life.

THE SPIRITUAL PERSPECTIVE

Detour Ending—the New Road Ahead

> **Romans 12:2:** "Do not conform to the pattern of this world, but be transformed by the renewing of your mind. Then you will be able to test and approve what God's will is—his good, pleasing and perfect will."

- What changes might I anticipate in my faith and belief system because of my grief journey? How will the "new road" I take in my life be different from the "old road"?

The End of Detour sign seemed like it would never come. But here it is. For the longest time you've been stuck between two semi-trucks driving slowly on a single-lane country road. Minutes seemed to pass as if they were hours. You're eager to get to your destination, but no one hurries. They don't seem to care about your needs or agenda. But now, relief is just ahead. A fresh ribbon of paved highway stretches before you on what was more like your original course, and you are eager to get back on your way.

That time will come on your grief detour as well. For the longest time you may have experienced all kinds of obstacles—certainly a slow down. But now you sense you are almost through it. What will it be like to put your life on cruise control once again and travel more easily on the highway of life?

Romans 12:2 is a classic passage on how to live day to day, especially appropriate for you because you are now ready to reinvest at the end of your grief detour. The passage has a warning, an invitation, and a challenge for you.

The *warning* is to watch out for the pitfalls. "Do not conform any longer to the pattern of this world." That can mean a lot of things, but especially for you it certainly means, "Don't expect your life to suddenly return to what it was before your loved one died." Something is now different—significantly different. Other people may not know or understand the changes you are facing. They'll expect you to get back into your old life.

But that can't happen. Some new things have to take its place.

The *invitation* is to transform your mind—to think about your life and the world differently. In many ways, God is giving you an opportunity to start fresh. This is a form of the "sabbatical" modeled after the Old Testament Year of Jubilee in which all debts were paid, slaves and prisoners were set free, and land was returned to its original owner (Lev. 25). God was saying, "It's time to have a new start." He says that to you today. You certainly didn't want this death to happen, but you may eventually see this as a gracious opportunity to think outside the box and reinvest in life in new and creative ways.

That is the *challenge*. We've been saying all along that God has plans and purposes for your life, even after someone close to you has died. It's time to find out more precisely what those plans are now. This passage tells you to put God's will to the test. Remember, trusting in God is not only an attitude, it is also an action. You trust God by *doing* something.

Notice also that God's will has three wonderful qualities. God's will is *good*—it has beneficial outcomes. God's will is *pleasing*—it satisfies your heart and soul. God's will is also *perfect*—it will never fail. That is why Jesus taught us all to pray, "Your will be done, on earth as it is in heaven" (Matt. 6:10). The time has come to get back on your reconstructed life's journey and travel as a new and enriched person. "Trust me," says your Lord. "Trust my will. You'll find it to be good, pleasing, and perfect."

Prayer: I know, dear Lord, that the new life I am beginning to experience is solid evidence of your working in me on this grief detour. I have come to appreciate your gracious presence, even though I often felt abandoned and alone in my grief. Help me yield even more completely to your will as I start to explore what you have in mind for my life now. Help me to step out more fully in faith. *Amen*

Where Have All the People Gone?

Romans 12:13: *"Practice hospitality."*

Acts 10:34–35: *"I [Peter] now realize how true it is that God does not show favoritism but accepts those from every nation who fear him and do what is right."*

- How do I manage the changes in my relationships with others, especially within my social network and faith community? How do I reenter my faith community in a renewed way?

A very unexpected thing often happens as you continue to deal with your grief and begin to approach the end of your detour. You begin to realize that the way you relate to your friends (and how they relate to you) may have changed. The changes go in one of three directions. Some of your friendships may be closer and more intimate. Your relationships may have strengthened because of your grief journey. Other relationships may have become distant, weak, or even ended altogether. Perhaps you had been friends with people largely because of a connection you had through your deceased loved one. Now you may have very little in common with some of those people. The third thing that might happen is that you may have welcomed new people into your circle of relationships, perhaps those you have met on your grief detour.

As you begin to think more clearly about your relationships, remember that the Bible encourages us to keep our circle of friends open. "Practice hospitality," says Paul (Rom. 12:13). The apostle Peter received a vision of a sheet filled with the meat of all kinds of animals, and God ordered him to eat from all of them. Being a kosher Jew, he refused to eat the meat that was forbidden by Old Testament ritual law. But God said, "Do not call anything impure that God has made clean" (Acts 10:15). Peter later explained, "I now realize how true it is that God does not show favoritism" (Acts 10:34–35). As someone who is grieving, you may have to see people differently. You may decide to expand beyond your established, and perhaps somewhat closed, network of friends and see that God wants you to keep the front door of your social network wide open and hospitable to all.

So what might you specifically pray and work for when it comes to these dynamic, changing relationships? First, pray for the grace and insight to accept that a few people may no longer be as close to you as before. That will cause its own grief. Certainly talk with them about it, but if the relationship continues to fade, remember that not all friendships (even under normal circumstances) last a lifetime.

Second, pray and work at strengthening the relationships that do continue. Meaningful relationships are in direct proportion to your mutual willingness to communicate on a deeper level. The Bible encourages that kind of intimacy, urging us to pray for one another, encourage one another, and even forgive one another.

Third, pray and work at developing new friendships. These may be with people who have had experiences similar to yours. Join with others who have also experienced the comfort of Christ walking with them through their tragedy.

Finally, pray that Christ himself will be a closer friend. Find comfort by spending time in his Word, in prayer, and in service in his name. While we hope you have confidence that Christ raised your deceased loved one to new life in him, also have the confidence that Christ will raise you to a "new" life on earth.

Prayer: Dear Lord, I have now grieved not only the death of my loved one but also the changes in some of my relationships. But I thank you for those who have surrounded me with their love and support. You have provided strength through those who stayed close. I have also learned that you are a friend to those in need. Help me continue to find my place within my faith community and my social network. And help me reach out to be a friend to others. *Amen*

Take Up Your Bed and Walk

John 5:2–9: "Now there is in Jerusalem near the Sheep Gate a pool. . . . Here a great number of disabled people used to lie. . . . One who was there had been an invalid for thirty-eight years. When

Jesus saw him lying there and learned that he had been in this condition for a long time, he asked him, 'Do you want to get well?' 'Sir,' the invalid replied, 'I have no one to help me into the pool when the water is stirred. While I am trying to get in, someone else goes down ahead of me.' Then Jesus said to him, 'Get up! Pick up your mat and walk.' At once the man was cured; he picked up his mat and walked."

2 Corinthians 1:3–4: *"Praise be to the God and Father of our Lord Jesus Christ, the Father of compassion and the God of all comfort, who comforts us in all our troubles, so that we can comfort those in any trouble with the comfort we ourselves receive from God."*

- **Does wanting to get through the grief process make a difference in the outcome? While finding a new stride in my daily walk, how will I also find my renewed sense of purpose in Christ?**

What we find intriguing about the story of the lame man at the pool of Bethesda is the first question Jesus asks him: "Do you want to get well?" (John 5:6). What a silly question! We want to shout out for him: "Of course! I'm tired of being sick! I'm tired of trying!" But maybe the question isn't as rhetorical as it sounds. How can we say this kindly? Some people become accustomed to their sickness. They get used to it—this is the only life they know, and they seem unwilling to risk a change. The same is true for people who are grieving. Some slip into thinking that grief defines them. Or they want their past relationship with the deceased to define them. They never then get through their grief. They don't think that they can, or maybe a part of them doesn't really want to, so they make a decision not to let go. They may feel anxious, and so they hold on and get stuck.

Likewise, the question is a good one for you. Do *you* want to get well? Do *you* want to move out of your grief into a new life? If so, you have to face several challenges, the first of which is that you will need to redefine yourself one more time. When your loved one died, you were identified by yourself and by others as a griever. For a long time you probably were engrossed with grieving for what seemed to be twenty-four hours a day, seven days a week. With your identity as "the griever," you may have been like the man sitting by the pool. Part of him really wanted to get into the water, but he never had the energy or ability to do it by himself and didn't have anyone else to help him. So he learned to sit there for thirty-eight years!

Now Jesus comes to you with the same question. Do you want to get well? Do you? Be careful how you answer, because if you say yes, there is another challenge.

Along with redefining yourself, you will now have to do something else. "Pick up your mat and walk" was Jesus's command to the lame man. To you he may be saying, "Get up and invest in life." The time has come not only to say good-bye to your loved one but also to say good-bye to grieving as well. Move your grieving into the past. Remember it. Learn from it. But with work and faith you are freed from the constraints of grief, and you can actually get up and walk!

A third challenge will be managing other people's responses to your new life. Many will be happy for you, but some will question or challenge you. The paralyzed man likely faced those who wouldn't believe. "You're so different," people may say as you feel new energy surge through you, and you become involved in different interests and activities. "How can you get over the death of your loved one?" they may ask. "You will feel sad for the rest of your life" is what they may think should be the case.

But the miracle is in saying, "No, that isn't true. I can get *through* my grief by not trying to go around, over, or under it, but rather by facing it head on. There can be healing. God can give me a new life if I work with him in the process." Just as the lame man would always remember his years by the edge of the pool, you will remember your time with your loved one. You will be able to recall the pain of your grief. But you can still, with Christ's healing power, finally get up and walk.

The apostle Paul then adds one more challenge. He says that because of your painful grief experience, you may have a greater capacity for compassion and understanding to more effectively comfort others. You are hopefully better able to express empathy as you walk alongside other friends, members of your church, or family members when they face tough loss situations in their lives.

The miracle of healing the paralyzed man was instant and dramatic. The miracle of healing your grief will likely be a slow one. But listen for Christ whispering, "Do you want to get well?" Hopefully, each time your answer will be a little more decisively, "Yes!"

Prayer: My prayer, holy Father, is that I will choose with your help to get through my grief. As I begin to reinvest in life, please guide me to find a new place in all my relationships and in my life's direction. Most of all, help me find my hope in you, because I know that you alone are the one who can totally renew my strength. *Amen*

Seven

Taking Children Along on the Grief Journey

THE MENTAL HEALTH PERSPECTIVE

Helping Your Children with Their Grief While You Are Grieving

Parenting children into adulthood can be a wonderful experience, but that doesn't mean there aren't challenges along the way. This is particularly true when parents are grieving their own loss and have children who are also affected by that same death. Remember how your children once asked from the backseat of the car: "Are we there yet?" As the driver you had to focus on the detour while dealing with the impatience and maybe a bit of boredom of your children. The challenge of grieving also becomes a two-track process on the grief detour, because you need to help your children with their grief while also attending to your own. However, there may be times when your children are the very reason you keep going, because you *have to* take care of them.

In order for you to better understand how you can handle your own grief and your children's grief simultaneously, we want to discuss some primary premises of grief involving children, adolescents, and young adults. These premises provide the foundation on which to build support for your children and assist you on your detour through grief.

Understanding Younger Children's Perception of Death and Grief

Children and adolescents grieve differently than adults do. For one thing, they have fewer life experiences to draw on. Many other demographic factors and circumstances affect their responses as well. Their cognitive abilities are less refined, so their understanding of death is also less developed. Be aware that:

- *Children ages two and under* have no concept of death and usually imitate the behavior of the primary caretaker. If the caretaker cries frequently and is often absent, the infant will probably be more clingy and less likely to willingly follow their normal routine.

- *Children ages three to five* don't understand that death is permanent. They might expect to see the person who died return in the near future. They take seriously the terminology adults sometimes use when they say that the person is "gone" or "lost." They will expect that person to come home or be found. This age group also thinks that their wishes are so powerful and magical that they can make things occur. This may explain a child's guilt or regret if he or she had negative feelings toward the deceased or wished that person would die.

- *Children ages five through eight* perceive death in concrete terms connected to specific causes, such as he died because he was very, very, very sick, hurt, or old; or they believe a ghost, monster, goblin, or darkness played a role in the death.

- *Somewhere between the ages of eight and twelve* children begin to comprehend that death is a permanent biological process that is inevitable for all people. However, they don't think it will happen to them for a very long time because they are young. They are often most concerned about how the death will affect them with regard to their care and normal routines.

Understanding Adolescents' and Young Adults' Grief

- *With the onset of adolescence (ages thirteen through nineteen)* comes the ability to understand the future-oriented and abstract aspects of death, such as realizing that all the hopes and dreams they had for themselves connected to that deceased person have also ended. The self-protective mask of this age group is consistent with their pervasive sense of immortality and invulnerability to almost everything, including the possibility of their own death.

- *Young adults in their twenties* understand cognitively what death is but may be left feeling overwhelmed because of the emotional impact of the loss when they first encounter the death of someone close to them. However, they are so often preoccupied with intimacy and career issues at this age that these can significantly distract them at times from grieving.

Principles to Assist Children and Adolescents with Their Grief

Based on their observations, children and adolescents know that something bad has happened when a death occurs in their family. They are afraid of what this will mean for them. Death can involve a loss of a multitude of relationships. If a father died, an eight-year-old may wonder who will coach their soccer team. A teenage daughter whose mom died may say, "Oh no! Who will help me with guy issues?" No more outings are possible following the death of grandparents who often took time to listen and play with grandchildren. Or the death of a favorite aunt, uncle, or a best buddy ends those times of hanging out together.

Loss is a heart-wrenching event, and children and adolescents experience grief in many different ways, depending on a variety of individual factors. Sometimes adults make the error of writing children off as if they don't have any feelings—particularly if they are too young to be very expressive or if they seem to push their feelings inside. Don't make that mistake yourself.

Children and adolescents tend to postpone much of their grieving until they sense that their parents or significant others have stabilized and worked through the majority of their grief. They don't want to jeopardize the security and support these adults provide by creating extra stress that may decrease the adults' ability to cope with their own grief, much less to be there for them.

While adults tend to grieve more continuously and intensely, children, adolescents, and young adults often grieve in a sporadic or intermittent form because they are concurrently facing a multitude of developmental issues, pressures, and questions. Grief seems to be a much longer process for them as they tend to primarily focus on their day-to-day personal, educational, and social needs. However, at times they will experience a wave of grief when a significant event occurs without their deceased loved one (like a sports event, school activity, holiday, or special occasion). If you are a parent, realize that your child, adolescent, or young adult probably won't grieve nonstop, and may often behave as if he or she is unaffected by the death a good deal of the time. They, more so than adults, typically experience a grieve-retreat-grieve pattern on their grief journey.

If you are worried because your children and adolescents aren't outwardly expressing their grief, check that they aren't totally denying their loss. Ask them if they think about the person who died. But also remind yourself that the grief experience for children and young people is different than it is for adults.

Remember that children, adolescents, and young

adults may be encountering only their first or second significant loss experience with a loved one's death. This is new territory for them, difficult and painful as it may be. This may be the first time they emotionally realize that all people really do die (even younger people at times), and that it can happen within their close family circle. Adolescents are especially shocked when they awaken to the fact that they and others they love are not immune to death, are not indestructible, and don't live in a protective bubble. Death does occur in their lives too—not just to other people.

Just as young people learn driving rules and how to manage detours from their parents, so too they learn from parents how to manage this life detour of grieving. If you have grieving children, show them that it is all right to cry, feel sad, and talk about the person who died. Talk about what you miss or don't miss about that person. Let them know there may be times in their grieving when they won't want to do things because they seem overwhelming or purposeless. This may be all right for a short period of time, but help them understand that they will have to face their grief again at a later time. We hope that through your grieving process you can provide a model of healthy ways to manage grief.

Children, adolescents, and young adults also need to have their feelings and concerns normalized. Give them the message that it's okay to feel the way they do. This also means you can't protect your children from their pain or fix things for them. Let them learn it's okay to be angry, to have guilty or regretful feelings and a myriad of other emotions. Teach them how to express those feelings and work through them. You will be a gift to your children if you can be a nonjudgmental and supportive listener as well as helping them understand some things about grieving.

Learn what things are typical in children and young people who are on the grief detour, and know when to seek help from a professional specializing in grief and loss issues. One very serious situation is when a child or adolescent feels suicidal and has developed a plan to act on those feelings. Feeling as though he or she would like to die, or wishing they had died with the person, but they *do not* intend to take action on that feeling is different than active suicidal thoughts. It is not uncommon to wish one would die soon after a death. But ask the child or adolescent directly if this is a fleeting thought with no real intended action or meant as a serious threat, and if the latter, get help for him or her as soon as possible.

Another reason to get assistance from a counselor is if your child or adolescent develops academic problems. Approximately 20 percent of children and adolescents are unmotivated to apply themselves to schoolwork after a significant loss. They have difficulty focusing, concentrating, or finding a purpose to study. Be alert for other problematic signs such as using alcohol or drugs, misusing food, or self-mutilation in an attempt to ease the pain. Signs of persistent guilt or self-blame may lead to these self-destructive behaviors. In addition, watch for anger expressed in acting out aggressively toward others, severe anxiety or phobias, continuing physical or somatic complaints, or persistent difficulty in talking about the deceased person. Many times all that is needed to help a child or adolescent get back on a healthier track is an assessment by a mental health professional and subsequent counseling. Therapists frequently use play or talk therapy for a brief number of sessions with intermittent follow-up as necessary, depending on the needs of the young person.

Throughout the grieving process, provide your child or adolescent with your unconditional love and presence, as well as a commitment to help in whatever ways you can. Hopefully each year as they get a little older they will become more aware of their need to work through their significant loss issues. As children mature cognitively, they may ask questions anew, view the loss differently, and want to reopen a discussion with a parent or other adult that was thought to be handled completely in the past. It's important to allow for those questions or go over again how the death occurred (maybe years prior) and things about the deceased. At subsequent cognitive levels, children and adolescents can process information to do grief work that couldn't be processed at an earlier time. The goal, of course, is for them to eventually heal from the pain of their grief and be grateful for the time they had with their deceased loved one.

THE SPIRITUAL PERSPECTIVE

Robber? Murderer?

> *John 3:16:* "*For God so loved the world that he gave his one and only Son, that whoever believes in him shall not perish but have eternal life.*"

- **How can I help my children understand God's role in death and grief? Can they comprehend that God is neither a robber nor a murderer, even though he was aware that their loved one was dying?**

Adults have a hard enough time understanding God's role in evil. But for children, it may not make sense at all. How can it be that Jesus, who loves them, would let Grandpa or Mommy die? "Jesus loves me, this I know" is a song many children learn to sing when they are very young. But when someone in their family, or one of their friends, actually dies, all the questions come: "Why did Jesus let this happen?" "I thought he loved me and my family." Even if they realize that God can do anything, they may not understand that he *allows* but does not directly *cause* a person's death.

Help your children understand two main points about what the Bible teaches regarding God's role in death. The first point deals with "consequences." You may want to use an example of when they disobey a warning like "Don't touch the burner on a hot stove." There are natural consequences if they ignore the warning. You are disappointed and sad when they don't listen, but you can still be a caring person when they actually touch the stove (in spite of your warning) and burn their fingers. You didn't want them to do it, and you certainly didn't actually burn them yourself! The injury was the direct result of not listening to your warning of what would inevitably happen if they touched the hot stove.

When God told Adam and Eve not to eat from the Tree of the Knowledge of Good and Evil, he was giving them a similar warning. If they ate from that tree, there would be inevitable consequences. God didn't want them to eat from the tree, but he wouldn't personally kill them like a murderer. Death (like burning your fingers) was the direct consequence of the action they took.

The second point is that God could have made us like robots so he could control our every choice, and we would never make a mistake. But he didn't create us that way. He wanted us to *choose* to love and obey him, because choosing him would reveal our own personal desire to love him. If he forced us to do all he wanted, then it would only prove, as we already know, that he can control everything. So God created Adam and Eve with a free will to voluntarily choose to obey him. And we know the rest of the story. Once sin entered the world, God had no choice but to be just and follow through with what he had warned. Therefore, God doesn't *cause* death like a murderer or steal our loved one's life away like a robber, but rather he *allows* it to happen, as he explained he would, if we disobeyed.

Death is the result of our collective disobedience to God's warning through the action of Adam and Eve. But the story doesn't end there. That is just the beginning. God is so powerful that he made another plan to redeem us through his Son. He worked it out in such a way that only our physical bodies die; our souls go to be with God in heaven. If your child is thinking that God took their loved one (a robber!) or caused that person to die (a murderer!), help him or her understand the rest of the story. God is neither a robber nor a murderer. He is our Savior.

Prayer: Dear Father, friend of children, help my children understand your true loving nature. Help them see that you are the answer to our problems, not the cause. Give us the faith to see that even the worst of all situations—the disobedience of Adam and Eve—is conquered through the love of Christ. Help conquer our grief as well. *Amen*

Listen, and Then Say It Clearly

Matthew 18:3–6: *"Truly I tell you, unless you change and become like little children, you will never enter the kingdom of heaven. Therefore, whoever takes a humble place—becoming like this child—is the greatest in the kingdom of heaven. And whoever welcomes one such child in my name welcomes me."*

Mark 10:13–16: *"People were bringing little children to Jesus for him to place his hands on them, but the disciples rebuked them. When Jesus saw this, he was indignant. He said to them, 'Let the little children come to me, and do not hinder*

them, for the kingdom of God belongs to such as
these. Truly I tell you, anyone who will not receive
the kingdom of God like a little child will never
enter it.' And he took the children in his arms,
placed his hands on them and blessed them."

• **How can I respond to my children as Jesus did while I am grieving? How can I use healthy approaches in talking with my children about God, death, and loved ones?**

"Mom, why are you crying? What happened to Dad?" "When will we see Grandma again?" "What is dead?" "How long does it last?" "Doesn't Jesus love us anymore?" These are a few of the questions that children ask when they realize something awful happened in their family.

With preteens and adolescents, the withdrawal and silence might hang awkwardly in the air because of the huge chasm between their discomfort with death and expressing their feelings. The "I don't know" mumbled with a shrug says, "Don't get any closer—I don't want to let you in here!" or "This is too painful and confusing. I'm not going to try to figure it out right now."

The Bible often speaks about children, especially in Jesus's life and ministry. Two passages come to mind rather quickly. One is when Jesus tells his disciples that children are not a bother. They need to have as much access to Jesus as adults. The second is where Jesus says that we must all become like little children to inherit the kingdom of God. It's pretty clear that children are valuable to Christ. We need to deliberately take the time to listen to them, understand what they are saying, and answer their questions. Remember Job's friends? They were supportive while they sat and listened to him *until* they began to offer advice when it really wasn't wanted. A good rule, especially with children and adolescents, is to listen more than you speak.

Trying to take care of your children's emotional needs while dealing with your own is difficult. At times it feels like a juggling act. Your children may be acting out, crying, or withdrawing. They are hurting. So what would be the healthiest way for you to help them with their grief while you are grieving as well?

Jesus is telling us two specific things in these passages. First, don't push them away or ignore them. Jesus was very angry with his disciples when they did this. Second, really welcome them. Bring them into the conversation. Help strengthen their faith and help them understand how to grieve in a Christian manner.

Once you have opened up conversation with them, help them especially with their spiritual questions. Where is God anyway? Why did he allow this to happen to us? Is this a punishment for doing something bad?

Where is the person who died? Will I see that person in heaven? These questions are only the beginning of what children worry about or want to know. Talk directly and honestly, with genuine responses to reassure them. They will realize their concerns are normal, and that you are a safe place when they want to talk about their grief.

That is what Jesus meant, we believe, when he encouraged people to welcome children. The really difficult part is to do that even while you are grieving. Your children trust you to help them understand the truth about death and God. They can, in turn, become a model for you of how to have a childlike faith and trust that God will take care of all of you and make your lives better again. So, even in your grief, reach out to include your grieving children, and feel God's richest blessing in the process.

Prayer: Thank you, loving Father, for helping me see more clearly the way I should trust you through the example of children. Please help me give my children an accurate portrayal of your amazing love for us. I am as dependent on you for support as a small child is on a parent. I am your child. Bend down and hold me in your care. *Amen*

A Child's View of Heaven

> **John 14:3:** *"If I go and prepare a place for you, I will come back and take you to be with me that you also may be where I am."*

> **Revelation 21:1–2, 10–11:** *"Then I saw 'a new heaven and a new earth,' for the first heaven and the first earth had passed away, and there was no longer any sea. I saw the Holy City, the new Jerusalem, coming down out of heaven from God, prepared as a bride beautifully dressed for her husband. . . . And he carried me away in the Spirit to a mountain great and high, and showed me the Holy City, Jerusalem, coming down out of heaven from God. It shone with the glory of God, and its brilliance was like that of a very precious jewel, like jasper, clear as crystal."*

- **How do I present death and heaven to my children in a clear and precise way that doesn't sound like a fairy tale but is believable and true?**

"Once upon a time, long, long ago in a country very far away, there lived a lovely young princess in a large castle in the woods . . ." That's how a typical fairy tale begins. Children have vivid imaginations that readily accept as real things like talking animals, brave knights on white horses, and the secret potions of the Harry

Potter books. Fairy tales also usually involve some conflict or drama. The damsel is in distress until the hero comes to the rescue. Then they all live happily ever after.

The closing chapters of the book of Revelation sound a bit like a classic fairy tale. Actually, the entire Bible starts with "Once upon a time, before anything else existed, God created everything." As in a fairy tale, Adam and Eve lived in Paradise. But something terrible happened. As a human race, we (like the damsel in a fairy tale) were thrown into "distress." The hero—Jesus Christ—must come to our rescue. And when Christ returns, we will live happily ever after.

How do children know that the one story is make-believe and the other is the true story of this entire universe? That isn't as hard as it might seem. Very few children become teenagers still believing that Santa Claus or the Easter Bunny are real. They eventually see them as symbols of society's celebration of these events. But hopefully the other message they hear is that the story of Jesus is true. At the conclusion of our seeing Mel Gibson's movie *The Passion of the Christ*, someone jumped up, turned to the audience, and loudly said, "Please understand, this movie is not make-believe. It's not just another story. This really happened. Jesus is real!"

If our children know that we truly believe Jesus is real, then his home in heaven must be real too. We can't see heaven from here, and other people can't come back from there. Doris Stickney has a helpful little book entitled *Waterbugs and Dragonflies* to assist children in understanding this point.[6] The story helps children see that there is another reality (heaven) beyond this world that the waterbug can't get to until it becomes a dragonfly. Christians, of course, can add all the wonderful promises of Scripture to the story. Heaven is a realm we reach when we die, and we cannot have access to it beforehand.

When a loved one dies and your children are asking about heaven, we think it is important to assure them of four things. *First*, assure them that heaven is a real place. It is not a fantasy world—not an imaginary castle in some imaginary place. Heaven is God's home. This is the place where Jesus lives.

Second, assure them that Christians go to this real place because Jesus went there after his resurrection to specifically prepare a place *for them* (John 14:3).

Third, let them know that this place is so special and so different that we can't really see it from here, and those who go there can't come back—ever. But they are just fine! They are no longer sad, sick, weak, lonely, or afraid (Rev. 21:4).

Finally, let them know that all of us as Christians will go to heaven when we die. There is plenty of room in heaven for us. So even if we live a long, long time on earth, Jesus will still keep a reserved sign on the room he prepared especially for them and for you.

Prayer: I can hardly picture what heaven is like, dear Lord. You are the Almighty God, majestic beyond all my imagination. I thank you for helping me find peace and direction for my life now, but I am eager to join you in your eternal home. May I be able to convey to my children the grandeur of this special place prepared for us at the end of our earthly lives. *Amen*

The End of the Detour—
Making It to the Other
Side of Grief!

Often after being on a detour, we have a great sense of relief as we finally get back on the main route. The detour has ended. You are back on your intended course or on a good alternative. However, when your grief detour comes to an end, you will not be getting back on exactly the same road you were on originally. Remember that there is an old (past) normal and now a new (present) normal without your deceased loved one. You undoubtedly are more aware as you leave the grief detour that you didn't die along with your loved one. He or she made that journey alone. You are still alive, and you have the rest of your life ahead of you. You may not know what is ahead, but hopefully you realize that some good and special things await you. You hopefully now understand and believe that you are equally as valuable a person as your loved one was, with your own set of strengths. Put your value on an equal plane with his or her. Your loved one has completed life on earth, for as long or as short a time as that was, but your life is not over. You have more time here. Make the most of it. The crux of the matter is that you are responsible for living your own life with quality and integrity. Humanly speaking, life is a journey you complete for and with yourself.

So, are you the same person as the one who entered the detour? We would say: "Definitely not." Just like the waves of the sea polish the rocks they wash against, so grief smoothes out some of our rough spots. Grief causes growth like nothing else we know of. It reorders priorities and life values. It helps us appreciate the goodness of the smaller things found in each day, of children playing and nature all around. It often reduces the fear of our own dying because we've walked alongside our loved one and experienced his or her death.

For most of us who have been on this grief detour, the lessons learned are invaluable, never to be forgotten. They may not have been worth the price you had to pay, but you didn't have a choice in the matter. And you wouldn't voluntarily choose to do it again. The death of a loved one forced you onto a detour against your will. But as we know, death eventually happens to all of us, including those we love dearly. Death is ugly! But grief also provides opportunities for growth. Think about all the wisdom you have gained by going through this extremely difficult loss and grieving experience. We hope this little book—this road map for getting through your grief—will help you travel through your grief detour in a healthy manner as you learn to live again after the death of your loved one.

Susan J. Zonnebelt-Smeenge, R.N., Ed.D.
Robert C. DeVries, D.Min., Ph.D.
May 2006

Notes

1. Susan J. Zonnebelt-Smeenge and Robert C. DeVries, *The Empty Chair: Handling Grief on Holidays and Special Occasions* (Grand Rapids: Baker, 2001), 17.

2. Stephanie Ericsson, *Utne Reader* 47 (Sept.–Oct. 1991): 75–79.

3. One of the earliest and clearest expressions of task theory is that of J. William Worden in *Grief Counseling and Grief Therapy: A Handbook for Mental Health Practitioners*, 2nd ed. (New York: Springer, 1991), 10–18.

4. The acronym DEER was first suggested to us by Billie Humphrey, Aftercare Coordinator, K. L. Brown Funeral Home and Crematory, Jacksonville, Alabama.

5. Charles A. Corr, Clyde M. Nabe, and Donna M. Corr, *Death and Dying, Life and Living*, 3rd ed. (Belmont, CA: Wadsworth, 2000), 3.

6. Doris Stickney, *Waterbugs and Dragonflies: Explaining Death to Young Children* (Cleveland: Pilgrim Press, 2004).